Camouflage, Insignia and Tactical Markings of the Aircraft of Red Army Air Force in 1941

Volume 1

Mikhail Timin

Helion & Company

Helion & Company Limited
Unit 8 Amherst Business Centre
Budbrooke Road
Warwick
CV34 5WE
England
Tel. 01926 499 619
Email: info@helion.co.uk
Website: www.helion.co.uk
Twitter: @helionbooks
Visit our blog at blog.helion.co.uk

Published by Helion & Company 2023
Designed and typeset by Mach 3 Solutions (www.mach3solutions.co.uk)
Cover designed by Paul Hewitt, Battlefield Design (www.battlefield-design.co.uk)

Text © Mikhail Timin 2023. English translation © Helion & Company 2023
Images © Central Archive of the Ministry of Defense of the Russian Federation, Russian State Military Archive, State Archive of
Russian Federation, State Archive of Sverdlovsk region, Russian State Archive of Economics, Russian State Archive of Scientific and
Technical Documentation, Finnish Wartime Photograph Archive and Mikhail Timin.
Colour plates by by Alexander Kazakov, Sergey Trufanov and Vladimir Kamskiy © Mikhail Timin 2023

ISBN 9-78-1804512-56-2

British Library Cataloguing-in-Publication Data.
A catalogue record for this book is available from the British Library.

For details of other military history titles published by Helion & Company Limited contact the above address or visit our website:
http://www.helion.co.uk.

We always welcome receipt of book proposals from prospective authors.

Contents

List of Abbreviations   iv

Russian Archive Abbreviations and Document References   v

Introduction   vi

1   Camouflage of VVS RKKA Aircraft on the Eve of the Great Patriotic War   7

2   Aircraft Factory Painting – The First Official Camouflage Scheme and the First Impromptu Camouflages   50

3   VVS RKKA Aircraft Units: Application of Camouflages in Accordance With the Approved Scheme and Variety of Impromptu Paint Schemes   77

4   Shaping the Final Look: Black-and-Green Camouflage and Enlarged Insignia in Six Positions   124

5   Winter Camouflage   198

List of Abbreviations

BAD – Bomber Aviation Division (*Bombardirovochnaya Aviatsionnaya Diviziya*)
BAP – Bomber Aviation Regiment (*Bombardirovochniy Aviatsionniy Polk*)
IAD – Fighter Aviation Division (*Istrebitelnaya Aviatsionnaya Diviziya*)
IAK – Fighter Aviation Corps (*Istrebitelniy Aviatsionniy Korpus*)
IAP – Fighter Aviation Regiment (*Istrebitelniy Aviatsionniy Polk*)
LShAP – Light Ground-attack Aviation Regiment (*Lyogkoshturmovoy Aviatsionniy Polk*)
NII VVS – Air Force Scientific Testing Institute (*Naucho-Ispytatelny Institut Voyenno-Vozdushnykh Sil*)
NKAP – People's Commissariat of Aviation Industry (*Narodny Komissariat Aviatsionnoy Promyshlennosti*)
NKO – People's Commissariat of Defense (*Narodny Komissariat Oborony*)
RAP – Reconnaissance Aviation Regiment (*Razvedyvatelniy Aviatsionniy Polk*)
SAD – Composite Aviation Division (*Smeshannaya Aviatsionnaya Diviziya*)
SBAP – High-Speed Bomber Aviation Regiment (*Skorostnoy Bombardirovochniy Aviatsionniy Polk*)
SNK – Council of People's Commissars (*Sovet Narodnykh Komissarov*)
VIAM – All-Union Research Institute of Aviation Materials (*Vsesoyuzny Institut Aviatsionnogo Materialovedeniya*)
VVS RKKA – Workers' and Peasants' Red Army Air Force (*Voyenno-Vozdushniye Sily Raboche-Krestyanskoy Krasnoy Armii*)
ZAP – Reserve Aviation Regiment (*Zapasnoy Aviatsionniy Polk*)

Russian Archive Abbreviations and Document References

ЦАМО – Central Archive of the Ministry of Defense of the Russian Federation
РГВА – Russian State Military Archive
ГАРФ – State Archive of Russian Federation
ГАСО – State Archive of Sverdlovsk region
РГАЭ – Russian State Archive of Economics
РГАНТД – Russian State Archive of Scientific and Technical Documentation
ф. (фонд) – fund
оп. (опись) – register
д. (дело) – file
л. (страница) – page

Introduction

About twenty years ago a fundamental work by Vasily Vakhlamov and Mikhail Orlov was published in *M-Hobby* magazine; it was devoted to the camouflage of Soviet Air Force aircraft during the 1920-40s and relied on the enormous amount of information; however, given the photographic and documentary material available at the time, it failed to fully disclose all the details of the processes that occurred. This volume is devoted to a more comprehensive review of the camouflage variety, as well as tactical markings and insignia, applied to the aircraft of the Workers' and Peasants' Red Army Air Force (VVS RKKA, *Voyenno-Vozdushniye Sily Raboche-Krestyanskoy Krasnoy Armii*) in 1941.

The author would like to express his gratitude to Gennady Serov, Sergey Kuznetsov, Peter Zaika, Alexey Pekarsh, Sergey Chekunov, Oleg Kiselyov, Vitaly Timoshenko, and Gennady Sloutskiy for the provided assistance, photos, schemes and documents. When preparing this book, the author used documents and photos from the Central Archive of the Ministry of Defense of the Russian Federation, Russian State Military Archive, State Archive of Russian Federation, State Archive of Sverdlovsk region, Russian State Archive of Economics, Russian State Archive of Scientific and Technical Documentation, as well as from the personal archive of the author. Colour artwork by Alexander Kazakov, Sergey Trufanov and Vladimir Kamskiy.

Whilst preparing this book, the author selected documents and photos from the Central Archive of the Ministry of Defense of the Russian Federation, Russian State Military Archive, State Archive of Russian Federation, State Archive of Sverdlovsk region, Russian State Archive of Economics, Russian State Archive of Scientific and Technical Documentation, Finnish Wartime Photograph Archive, as well as from his personal archive.

1

Camouflage of VVS RKKA Aircraft on the Eve of the Great Patriotic War

It is common knowledge that the camouflage of military facilities and equipment in the Red Army was a matter of great importance. After the end of the Russian Civil War (1917-23) the issues of camouflage were thoroughly discussed and studied, which resulted in a series of changes in all armed forces of the country. The military aviation was involved as well. Along with developing the forms and methods of camouflaging airfields and various buildings, serious efforts were taken to make aircraft as invisible as possible both on the ground and in the sky. One of such methods was camouflage painting the requirements to which were changing continuously. However, theoretical work in this area did not result in any practical use of the camouflage. By the mid-1930s the following approach to painting combat aircraft had been formed: all-metal airplanes produced at aircraft factories of the People's Commissariat of Aviation Industry (NKAP, *Narodny Komissariat Aviatsionnoy Promyshlennosti*) and used by the VVS RKKA were painted mainly with silver or light grey enamels. Aircraft made of wood or mixed construction should be painted with green aircraft dope/lacquer (*aerolac*) on the upper surfaces and silver on the undersides.

Insignia in the form of a red five-pointed star with black edging were applied in six positions (fuselage, upper and lower surfaces of each wing). Tactical markings were applied in accordance with the *Rules for application of identification marks and ciphers on military aircraft of the VVS RKKA* (see Chapter 6).

That's exactly how the NKAP required that the aircraft be painted in the early 1938. In January 1938 military representatives at NKAP aircraft factories received an order from Military Engineer 2nd rank Okulov, the then Head of the 1st Department of the VVS RKKA Material and Technical Supply Directorate, to accept only the aircraft painted in strict accordance with the following schemes:

1. *For land-based aircraft of wooden and mixed construction including trainer aircraft:*
    a) *lower surfaces of wings (both upper and lower wings of biplanes), lower surface of horizontal empennage and lower surfaces of fuselages (both faceted and monocoque) – to be painted in silver aluminum (matt) colour;*
    b) *upper surfaces of wings (both upper and lower wings of biplanes), upper surface of horizontal empennage, vertical empennage, upper surfaces of fuselages (both faceted and monocoque) – to be painted in 'protective'* (green with yellowish tinge – Translator's note) *colour;*
2. *For land-based metal aircraft:*
    a) *land-based metal aircraft to be painted entirely in silver-aluminum (matt) colour;*
3. *For naval aircraft of all designs:*
    a) *all naval aircraft (both flying boats and float planes) to be painted entirely in silver-aluminum (matt) colour.* (1)

In fact, this document formalized the practice that had existed since at least 1936. However, this camouflage scheme was not completely satisfactory to the Air Force and was soon changed. Already in the following year of 1939, some changes were apparently implemented into this order of painting. Despite the fact that I-153 fighters and R-10 multi-purpose airplanes had mixed and wooden construction, they were painted with AII light grey and silver AII aircraft lacquers at Factories Nos.1 and 292.

In addition, in some VVS RKKA units, the aircraft of mixed construction, originally painted at the factories in green ('protective') colour, were repainted in silver or light grey for some unclear reasons.

Later, according to the Directive No.220cc issued by the Defense Committee on 23 May 1940 and the NKAP Order No.228c issued on the same date, the VVS RKKA aircraft completed after 25 May 1940 were to be painted only in two colours: green on the upper surfaces and blue on the undersides. Painting in other colours was prohibited.

For covering the wooden and percale surfaces, the aircraft lacquers of second coating AII ('protective' green and light-blue) were approved; metal surfaces were to be painted with glyptal-based enamels: light green – A-19f [A19ф] and light blue – A-18f [A18ф].

The factories that had previously produced aircraft painted in noble shades of silver switched to a green-blue colour scheme; however, the aircraft in Air Force units kept their original colours. Among the exceptions there were factory-repaired aircraft, repainted according to a new scheme. Moreover, in some regiments, the silver-grey aircraft were covered with small spots and dashes of green, in the manner of camouflage used during the combats with the Japanese army at the Khalkhin-Gol River in summer 1939. Apparently, there were no strict requirements to unify the appearance of aircraft directly in the Air Force units, so usually a regiment could have aircraft painted in the factory or after repair in the 'new' green-blue standard, and the airplanes painted according to an improvised 'Khalkhin-Gol' scheme, or those remaining in the 'old' light grey or silver (aluminum) paint.

Reviewing the photos of wrecked SB bombers from the 24th High-Speed Bomber Aviation Regiment (SBAP, *Skorostnoy Bombardirovochniy Aviatsionniy Polk*) taken in spring 1941, it can be noted that the aircraft were painted both according to the new and old schemes. (2)

The I-153 fighters of the 160th IAP were either painted at the factory in the 'new' green-blue camouflage or in the improvised 'Khalkhin-Gol' scheme or remained in the 'old' light grey one. This can be clearly seen in the photos of the aircraft damaged by Luftwaffe at Minsk airfield of Loshchitsy on 24–25 June 1941 (3).

Aircraft with the so-called 'Khalkhin-Gol' scheme, as a rule, were painted quite freely – the paint was applied in those places of the aircraft where the personnel managed to get without much trouble. It is clearly visible on the example of I-153 s/n 6848 from the 4th IAP that crashed on 25 March 1941. Note that the upper surfaces of the wings are practically not covered with camouflage (4).

Most likely there existed the Air Force units with all aircraft painted in the 'Khalkhin-Gol' colour camouflage. Judging by photos, all or practically all SB aircraft of the 48th SBAP were painted in this way. (5)

Interestingly, there also existed a reverse process. Thus, in 1940, in the Central Asian Military District Air Force, the I-16 and I-15bis fighters were initially painted with standard AII 'protective' green and AII light blue aircraft lacquers; however, in the regiments they were repainted with silver (aluminum) AIIAl aircraft lacquer. The reason for this has not yet been clarified: probably, the aircraft were repainted into silver colour to prevent them from overheating in the sun.

However, the military were not originally satisfied with the paint samples available at the time because those paints were glossy, gave a strong glare, and failed to ensure the required camouflaging effect. In addition, it quickly became clear that the paintwork on the SB and DB-3f airplanes just released from the factories, painted with glyptal-based enamels A-19f, was not sufficiently resistant to the elements. The paint quickly became blurry and discoloured; it began to peel and crack in places of riveted joints. In autumn 1940 the factories were flooded with complaints from the Air Force units, which demanded eliminating the coating defects. Up until the spring of 1941 those requests were unhurriedly satisfied in compliance with the existing warranty obligations. (7)

The solution was found in developing and launching production of new paint types. Casein-based easy-to-wash paints developed by engineer V.V. Chebotarevskiy failed the field tests and were rejected; however, their tinting suggested by Chebotarevskiy later became the basis for the new nitro lacquers and oil enamels. At the same time the camouflage department within the Scientific Research Institute of Engineering Equipment of the Red Army developed a set of multi-colour disrupting (camouflage) aircraft paint schemes, which, unfortunately, were not implemented in practice.

Already by early 1941, a line of new paints appeared, including oil enamels intended for metal parts and surfaces, and nitro paints intended for wooden and percale surfaces. The nomenclature was initially represented by seven colours, numbered from 1 to 7: 1 – light brown, 2 – grey, 3 – 'yellow' (light green), 4 – green, 5 – dark green, 6 – achromatic (black), 7 – grey-blue.

The first batch of the new green paint, apparently of oil enamel AM-24, was released in February; the VVS RKKA headquarters immediately requested the 1st Main Directorate of the NKAP painting of four Pe-2 prototypes at Factory No.22 (8). Interestingly, it seems that at some point, in order to be on the safe side, it was decided to test the imported paints along with domestic ones. On 27 March Lieutenant General Astakhov ordered Major General Filin to paint 50 planes at each of the Factories Nos.1, 22, 292, 301, 381 and 387 with imported paints and varnishes, which were named in the documents as 'iharole' and 'herboloid' (9). Unfortunately, the outcome of this story is unknown, but it is highly likely that the paints were simply not purchased.

Taking into account the experience gained in the previous period, it was decided to continue the search for optimal camouflage. The process was initiated by an Order of the People's Commissariat of Defense (NKO, *Narodny Komissariat Oborony)* dated 27 December 1940, which demanded submitting proposals of the camouflage schemes by 10 January 1941. However, it was obviously impossible to obtain well researched material within such a short time. Nevertheless, the work was being done, and on 4 April, the Head of the 10th Directorate of the NKAP Tarasevich sent a telegram to the Head of the 1st Department of the 6th Main Directorate of the Air Force, Brigade Engineer Osipenko, saying that 50 aircraft produced at Factory No.22 would receive an experimental camouflage painting. (10)

In accordance with the Directive No.53cc of the Defense Committee within the Council of People's Commissars (SNK, *Sovet Narodnykh Komissarov)* of 29 April 1941, the NKAP was ordered to switch to a disrupting (camouflage) aircraft painting, as the most satisfactory with the camouflage requirements. Manufacturers had to make the corresponding arrangements and commencing from 1 October 1941 to switch to the production of all aircraft with camouflage painting of the upper and side surfaces and light grey colour undersides. And starting from 15 July 1941 the airplanes had to be covered with nondescript (matte) green paint instead of plain green one.

In order to finalize the paining variants, composition and durability of the paints, the NKAP was ordered to provide the NKO by 15 June 1941 an experimental batch of 100 aircraft (50 fighters and 50 bombers) painted in three-colour camouflage scheme in accordance with the technical requirements of the Air Force Main Directorate. Then, basing on the results of operating this experimental batch at the Air Force units, by September 1941 it was planned to develop the final technical requirements to the camouflage painting.

According to the report of the military representative of the Factory No.22, the nondescript paint was used for the first time in May 1941 when seven Pe-2s were painted. (11) Unfortunately, the paint type number is not mentioned in the document; most likely it was AM-24 enamel. (The whole range consisted of six paints: AM-21, AM-22, AM-23, AM-24, AM-25, and AM-26).

Aircraft painting in experimental camouflage schemes was started in June. Complete information about this work was not yet collected; however, judging by indirect data, the task was assigned to Factory No.21 for fighters and to Factory No.22 for bombers (possibly, in addition, the Factory No.153 was instructed to paint experimental camouflage on UTI-4 training aircraft).

Joint Act issued by Factory No.21 and All-Union Research Institute of Aviation Materials (VIAM, *Vsesoyuzny Institut Aviatsionnogo Materialovedeniya*) stated the following information about the painting of 50 LaGG-3 fighters with new nitro paints. Despite the requirement to cover the aircraft with nondescript paints, both the matte nitro paints (AMT-1, AMT-2, AMT-3, AMT-4, AMT-5, AMT-6), and the glossy ones (AGT-1 [АГТ-1], AGT-2 [АГТ-2], AGT-3 [АГТ-3], AGT-4 [АГТ-4], AGT-5 [АГТ-5], AGT-6 [АГТ-6]) were used.

Five camouflage schemes proposed by the Main Directorate of the Air Force were originally suggested for painting, respectively: variant Nos.1, 1a, 2, 2a, and 3. (12)

By 22 June 1941, all together five airplanes and 20 sets of wings had been painted, after which the factories switched to black-and-green camouflage.

Variant No.1 was the most widely used. Three LaGG-3 s/ns 3121376, 3121380, 3121387 were painted in accordance with this scheme. Variant No.2a was applied to the fighter s/n 3121377 and variant No.3 – to s/n 3121378. Apparently, there was no opportunity to paint any aircraft in accordance with variants 2 and 1a.

At least two aircraft – s/n 3121376 (variant No.1) and s/n 3121377 (variant No.2a) were painted with glossy AGT paints. As for the remaining aircraft, unfortunately, the report does not specify which paints – AGT or AMT – were used. It was noted that all the paints were easily sprayed with a spray gun; with viscosity of 6-8 they had normal spill and coverage properties. Paint consumption for variant No.1 was as follows: AGT-1 – 8.5 kg, AGT-4 – 11.0 kg, AGT-6 – 9.5 kg. For variant No.2a: AGT-2 – 8.0 kg, AGT-3 – 9.0 kg, AGT-5 – 9.0 kg. The colour boundaries produced by the spray gun (round jet) were clear and even, and insignificant roughness (overspray) at the edge between the colours was almost completely eliminated by wiping with a suede cloth. During painting it turned out that the side views on the provided schemes did not match the plan views, but this shortcoming was easily corrected – the schemes were adjusted on the spot. (13)

It should be noted that the fate of the five painted aircraft was different. Two planes each were sent to the Air Force Scientific Testing Institute (NII VVS, *Naucho-Ispytatelny Institut Voyenno-Vozdushnykh Sil*) and the 2nd ZAP, and a single LaGG-3 s/n 3121378, painted according to variant No.3, was sent to the combat regiment – the 24th IAP within the 6th Fighter Aviation Corps (IAK, *Istrebitelniy Aviatsionniy Korpus*) of Moscow Air Defense Forces. The airplane was lost as early as on 21 July 1941, on a mission to intercept an enemy plane. The pilot, Hero of the Soviet Union, Squadron Commander Captain G.M. Sokolov died. (14)

While only a small number of fighters were painted in three-colour camouflage, the situation with bombers was quite different. Factory No.22 was in the lead, and in June 1941 this factory managed to camouflage 71 Pe-2s. (15) Unfortunately, the report of the factory's military representative doesn't say how many of those aircraft got three-colour camouflage painting, and which camouflage variants were applied. However, there is no doubt that at least 50 Pe-2s got a three-colour camouflage. So far no documents like the act of VIAM and Factory No.21 have been found, so the theme of Pe-2 three-colour camouflage is not completely clear. However, there are many photos from photo albums of German soldiers which show that there were at least two or three camouflage schemes of the Pe-2s, similar to the ones which were used for the LaGG-3s. In addition, the aircraft produced after 20 June, in accordance with the NKO Directive, were given a new scheme for positioning the insignia stars in four locations. Taking into account that 50 planes of Factory No.22 were scheduled to be painted in camouflage scheme even before the NKO Directive of 29 April, and the existence of numerous German photos with the Pe-2s painted in three-colour camouflage, it is possible that about 100 planes which fought at the front line from Vitebsk to Odessa actually received the camouflage painting. There is a hope that the documents and painting schemes of Pe-2 can still be found in archives and this undoubtedly interesting story will be subsequently disclosed in a separate publication.

In addition to the factories which produced combat aircraft, the Factory No.153 in Novosibirsk, which at that time was building UTI-4 trainers, also received the order to paint an unknown number of airplanes in experimental camouflage scheme. According to the report of the military representative, the factory had no new paints at all, and before 15 July it was not possible to get new supplies; however, that didn't become an obstacle to the factory workers, who fulfilled the order.

As early as on 27 June, the factory personnel began applying a camouflage in the form of patches of black and sandy colour over the basic green colour. There are no types of the paints recorded in the documents, but it seems that they used AII aircraft lacquer of tobacco colour, and the black could be either AII aircraft lacquer or MV-109 [MB-109], or MV-6 [MB-6]. And on 1 July the first 11 freshly painted aircraft were shipped from Novosibirsk to Volsk, Kursk and Ryazan. Unfortunately, there is no exact information on the number of planes painted in three-colour camouflage in the reports of military representative of the Factory No.153. In July they accepted 55 UTI-4s, and it is not clear when the factory turned to applying the black-and-green camouflage. In August the last 12 aircraft were accepted, and the factory began building LaGG-3s, which were painted only in two-colour camouflage. (16)

Judging by some photos taken by the German servicemen at Shatalovo airfield in summer 1941 there is a small probability that the three-colour camouflage had been applied to some Il-2 airplanes: however, due to the small number of photos and lack of evidence in the documents published for the time being, this topic also needs additional research.

Interestingly, in addition to Factory No.153, whose directors were obviously not encouraged by the task they received, there was another enterprise that began experiments with camouflage painting of airplanes; apparently they did it on their own initiative, so to speak it was over the plan. It was the experimental Factory No.115 of A.S. Yakovlev Design Bureau. For the first time, camouflage painting was applied on a prototype two-seat fighter trainer UTI-26-I. The works were completed at the end of June – beginning of July 1940.

Judging by the photos taken in the course of the state tests which took place on 23–25 July, the airplane was originally painted in two-colour camouflage, which had a green background with black spots of the characteristic geometric shape. The reason for those actions, according to the documents, has not yet been clarified. Presumably, it was an initiative of VIAM, which, however, is doubtful. But given the context of the events, particularly the impact of Yakovlev's trip to Germany as part of the procurement committee, and the purchase of German airplanes, which were delivered to Moscow and based at Moscow Central airfield, it could be assumed that there was an attempt to replicate the German colour scheme. In fact, a specific variant of camouflage application, remotely resembling the scheme used for early Luftwaffe Bf 109E, indirectly points out to the German trace. It should be noted that later on this camouflage scheme was used on all aircraft prototypes built at Factory No.115, including I-28, I-30 and Yak-7 M-82. Moreover, the most mysterious aspect is the fact that the first series Yak-7 fighters manufactured by Factory No.301 in April–June 1941 (by 19 June, 26 airplanes had been accepted), also received this paint scheme, thus becoming the first series-built airplanes in the VVS RKKA painted in two-colour camouflage. And it seems that this was the initiative of the factory management, apparently not coordinated with the Air Force. A report to the Major General of Aviation Volodin from the acting Head of 10th Department of the Air Force Main Directorate Piskunov states: *The Yak-7 airplanes (high-speed fighter trainer) supplied to the Main Directorate of VVS RKKA by Factory No.301, basing on the drawings issued by the aircraft Chief Designer comrade Yakovlev, are camouflaged in black colour on the basic green background. Please inform me of your considerations on the expediency of camouflaging the Yak-7 airplane.* (17)

Additionally, such camouflage was probably intended to be used for painting the series I-26 fighters, which is indirectly confirmed by the painting scheme found by S.D. Kuznetsov in the archives of Yakovlev Design Bureau, where the I-26 (Yak-1 of the early series) is easily recognizable.

Since Yakovlev was then a Deputy of the People's Commissar of Aviation Industry, the camouflage scheme prepared by Factory No.115 was probably subsequently used in the painting not only of aircraft designed by Yakovlev, but also of the airplanes of other design bureaus, the more so as the two-colour camouflage had practical advantages over the three-colour one, as it was stated in the act of VIAM and Factory No.21: *'Application of the three-colour system of distorting camouflage insignificantly increases the labor intensity and duration of painting works; however, it requires an increase in the number of compressors, hoses and spray guns as related to the number of paint colours ...'* (18)

Nevertheless, the three-colour camouflage was eventually used for painting the planes of the VVS RKKA, but only since 1943. It should be noted that the first variants of this camouflage, which were not approved, almost completely replicated the paint schemes of the three-colour camouflages of 1941. (19)

List of documents employed:
1. ЦАМО, ф.4610, оп.1, д.170.
2. ЦАМО, ф.35, оп.11294, д.185, л.65–113, 309–329.
3. ЦАМО, ф.35, оп.11294, д.187, л.230–252.
4. ЦАМО, ф.35, оп.11294, д.195, л.266–279.
5. ЦАМО, ф.35, оп.11294, д.51, л.78–93.
6. ЦАМО, ф.35, оп.11294, д.199, л.127–141, 157–174.
7. ЦАМО, ф.35, оп.11287, д.44, л.71, 73–74.
8. ЦАМО, ф.35, оп.11287, д.44, л.153.
9. ЦАМО, ф.35, оп.11287, д.29, л.208.
10. ЦАМО, ф.35, оп.11287, д.29, л.207.
11. ЦАМО, ф.35, оп.11287, д.16, л.182.
12. ЦАМО, ф.35, оп.11287, д.83, л.268–275.
13. Ibid.
14. ЦАМО, ф.35, оп.11294, д.57, л.111–114.
15. ЦАМО, ф.35, оп.11287, д.16, л.205.
16. ЦАМО, ф.35, оп.11287, д.5, л.251–252.
17. ЦАМО, ф.35, оп.11287, д.78, л.104.
18. ЦАМО, ф.35, оп.11287, д.83, л.268–275.
19. ЦАМО, ф.69, оп.12144, д.1021, л.2–4, 11–13.

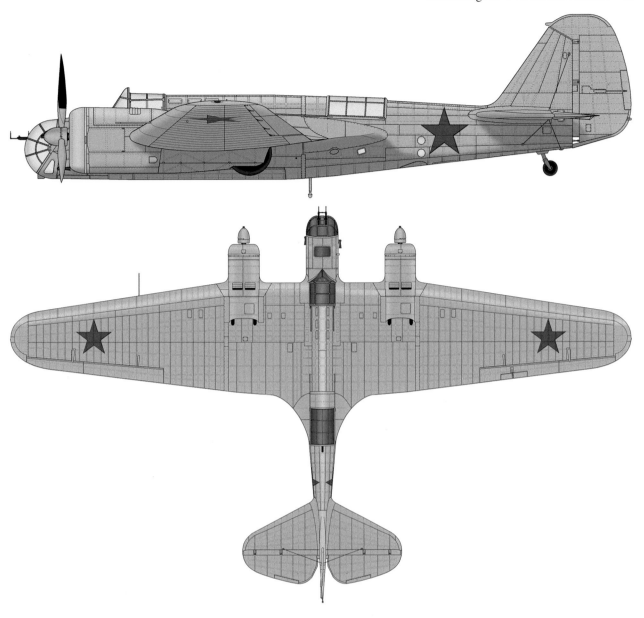

All-metal aircraft were painted entirely in a silver colour. SB bomber produced by Factory No.22, painted with AE-8 [АЭ-8] enamel.

SB bombers of the VVS RKKA. The planes are painted with AE-8 enamel.

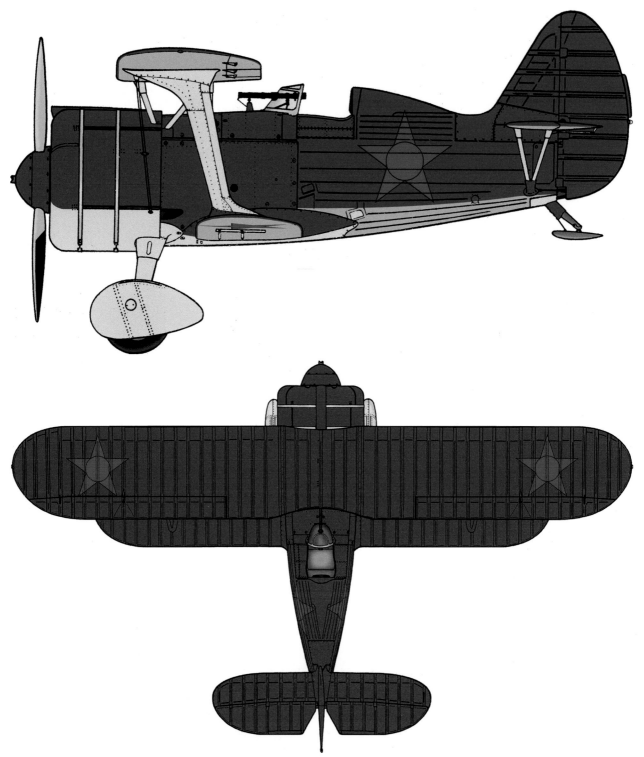

Above: Aircraft of mixed construction were painted according to the scheme: green on upper surfaces, silver undersides. I-15bis fighter was painted with aircraft lacquers: AII green ('protective') upper surfaces and AIIAl [AIIAл] silver (aluminum) undersides.

Left: I-15bis from the 55th Fighter Aviation Regiment (IAP, *Istrebitelniy Aviatsionniy Polk*) destroyed by Luftwaffe at Beltsi airfield. It is clearly visible that the undersides of the fuselage and wings are painted with AIIAl silver (aluminum) aircraft lacquer.

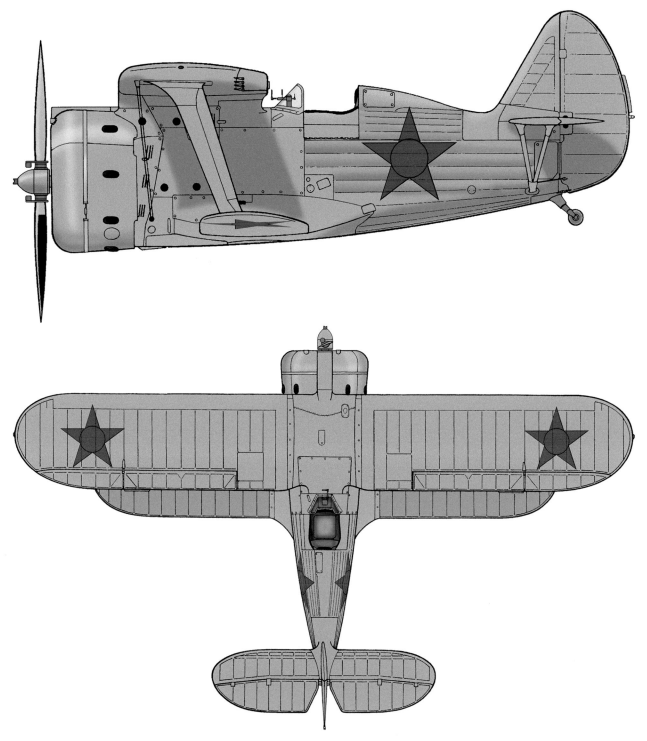

I-153 was painted with silver (aluminum) AIIAl aircraft lacquer.

I-153 was painted with silver (aluminum) AIIAl aircraft lacquer.

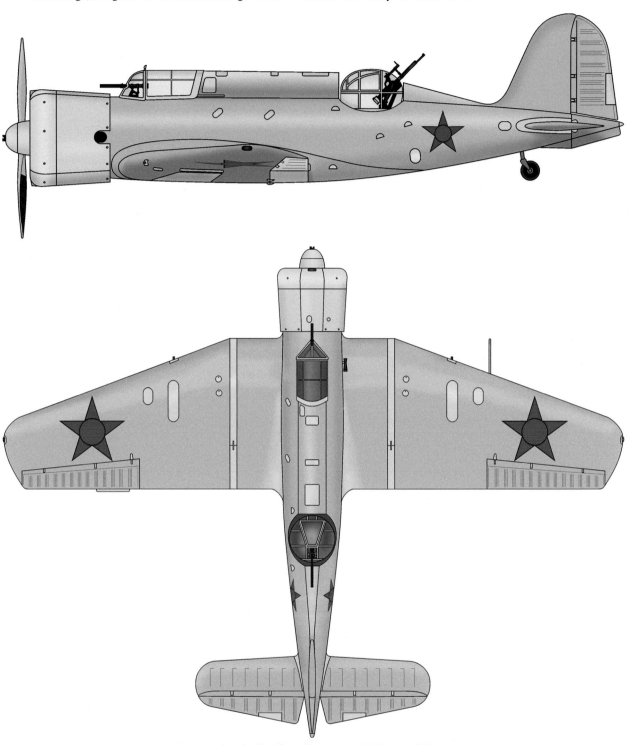

R-10 was painted with silver (aluminum) AIIAI aircraft lacquer.

R-10 of the 316th RAP, Proskurov airfield, summer 1941.

R-10 of the 316th RAP, Proskurov airfield, summer 1941.

R-10 was painted with silver (aluminum) AIIAl aircraft lacquer.

R-10 of the 316th Reconnaissance Aviation Regiment (RAP, *Razvedyvatelniy Aviatsionniy Polk*), captured by German troops at Proskurov airfield, summer 1941. Aircraft was painted with silver (aluminum) AIIAl aircraft lacquer.

R-10 of the 2nd Light Ground-attack Aviation Regiment (LShAP, *Lyogkoshturmovoy Aviatsionniy Polk*), damaged during emergency landing in 1939. The aircraft was painted with silver (aluminum) AIIAl aircraft lacquer.

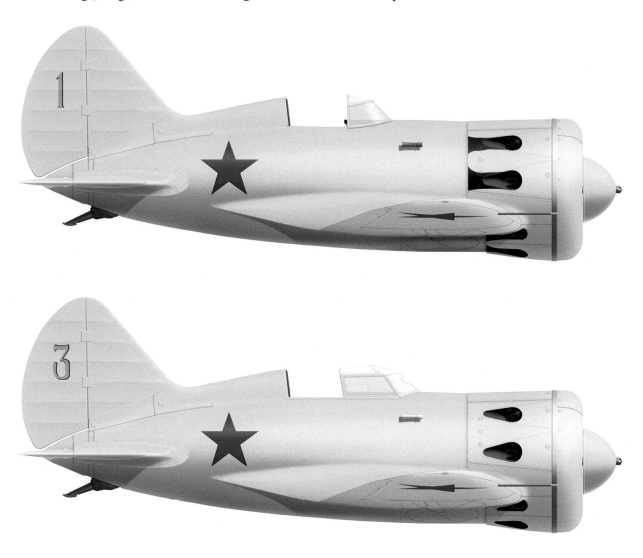

I-16s type 5 of the 33rd IAP, Pruzhany airfield, June 1941.

I-16s type 5, tactical numbers 1 and 3, of the 33rd IAP, captured by German troops at Pruzhany airfield, June 1941. Both aircraft were repainted with silver (aluminum) AIIAl aircraft lacquer.

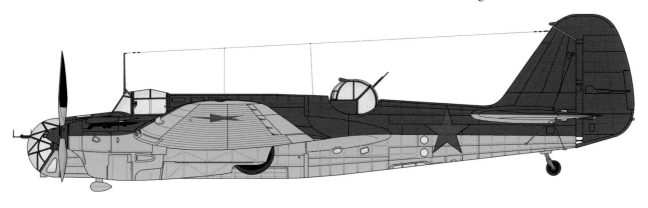

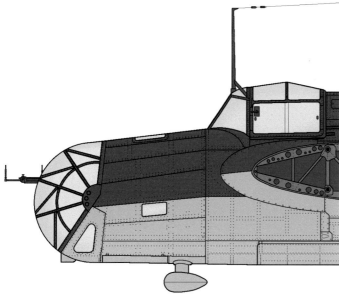

SB bombers built by Factory No.22, since May 1940 (starting with aircraft s/n 19/294) were painted in accordance with the new scheme – green on upper surfaces, blue undersides, using glyptal-based enamels (light green – A-19f, and light blue – A-18f).

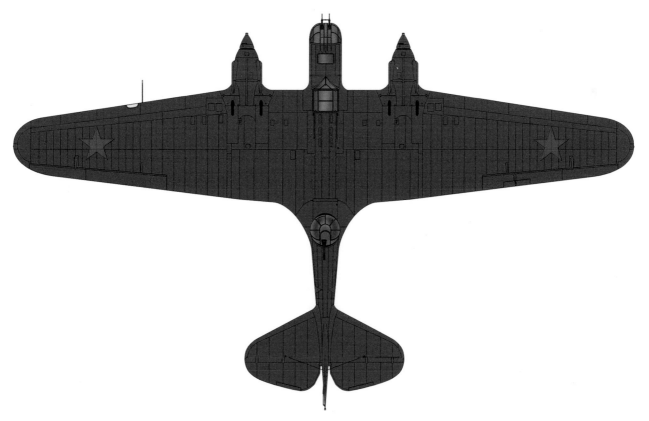

I-15bis s/n 5324, from the Staff Flight of the 106th Ground-attack Aviation Regiment (ShAP, *Shturmovoy Aviatsionniy Polk*) of the Central Asian Military District Air Force. Photo from accident report of 15 February 1941. The aircraft was repainted with silver (aluminum) AII Al aircraft lacquer.

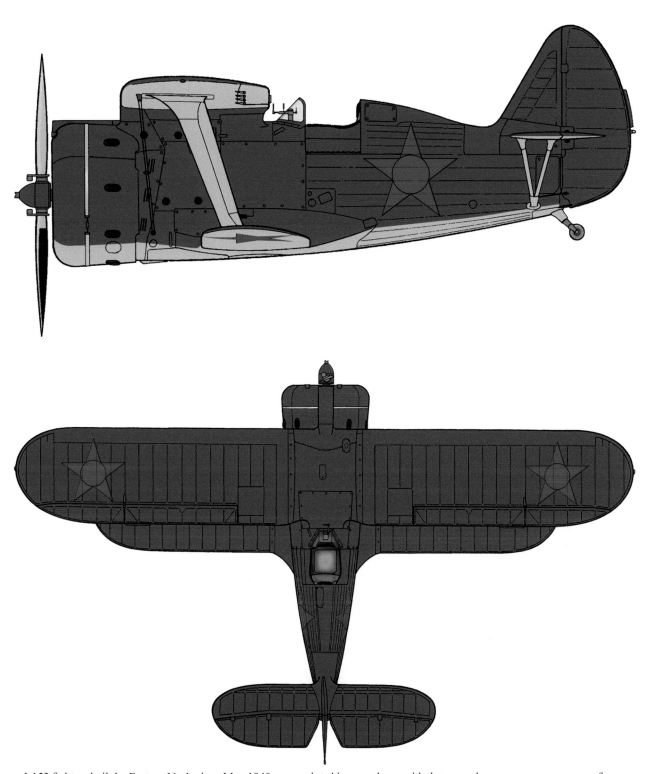

I-153 fighters built by Factory No.1, since May 1940 were painted in accordance with the new scheme – green on upper surfaces, blue undersides, using aircraft lacquers (AII 'protective' green and AII light blue).

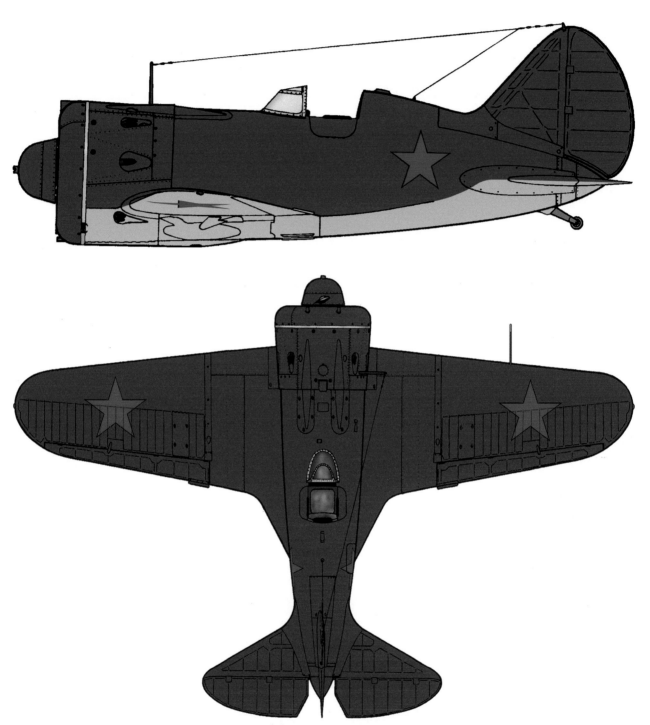

I-16 fighters built by Factory No.21, since May 1940 were painted in accordance with the new scheme – green upper on surfaces, blue undersides, using aircraft lacquers (AII 'protective' green and AII light blue).

SB bomber s/n 12/220 of the 24th SBAP.

This SB bomber s/n 12/220 of the 24th SBAP after repairs was painted in accordance with the new scheme – green on upper surfaces, blue undersides (light green – A-19f, and light blue – A-18f).

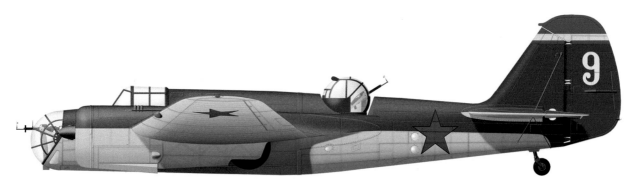

SB bomber s/n 19/70 of the 24th SBAP.

SB bomber s/n 19/70 of the 24th SBAP after repairs was painted in accordance with the new scheme – green on upper surfaces, blue undersides (light green – A-19f, and light blue – A-18f).

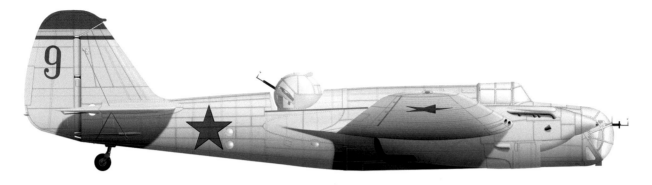

SB bomber s/n 8/217 of the 24th SBAP.

SB bomber s/n 8/217 of the 24th SBAP remained in standard colour of AE-9 light grey enamel.

I-153 of the 160th IAP.

I-153 of the 160th IAP, tactical number 16, was painted according to the so-called 'Khalkhin-Gol' scheme – irregularly shaped green spots against a light grey or silver basic background.

I-153 of the 160th IAP.

I-153 s/n 8030, tactical number 6, of the 160th IAP. This was one of the last aircraft manufactured by Factory No.1, and was painted according to the earlier scheme, using AII light grey aircraft lacquer.

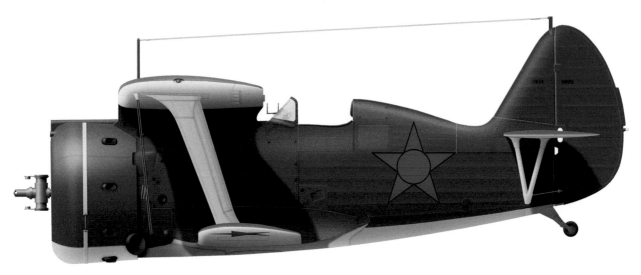

I-153 of 160th IAP.

I-153 manufactured in summer of 1940, which belonged to the 160th IAP, was painted under the Directive No.220cc issued by the Defense Committee and the NKAP Order No.228c of 23 May 1940, in accordance with the following scheme: green on upper surfaces, blue undersides, using aircraft lacquers (AII 'protective' green and AII light blue).

I-153 s/n 6848 of the 4th IAP, which crashed on 25 March 1941.

SB bomber of the 48th SBAP, Russka-Zhenska airfield.

SB s/n 3/115 from the 5th Squadron of the 48th SBAP was painted in accordance with the so-called 'Khalkhin-Gol' scheme – green spots of irregular shape, against the light grey AE-9 [АЭ-9] or silver AE-8 [АЭ-8] basic background.

SB bomber destroyed by Luftwaffe at Russka-Zhenska airfield (Lvov). The aircraft belonged to the 48th SBAP and was painted in accordance with the so-called 'Khalkhin-Gol' scheme – green spots of irregular shape on a light grey AE-9 or silver (aluminum) AE-8 basic background.

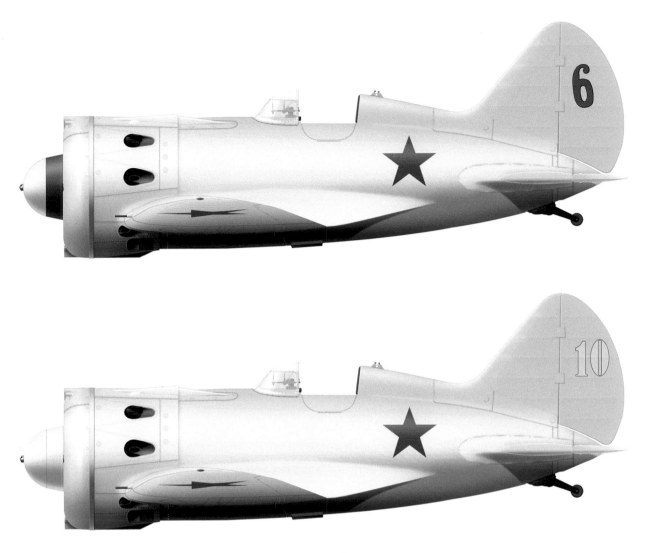

I-16s type 24 of the 116th IAP, May 1941.

Above and overleaf: I-16 type 24 s/n 2421Д-8, tactical number 6, from the 1st Squadron of the 116th IAP and I-16 type 24 s/n 2421Д-31, tactical number 10, from the 2nd Squadron of the 116th IAP, May 1941. Both aircraft were repainted with silver (aluminum) AИAl aircraft lacquer, although originally they were painted with standard AII protection green and light blue (6).

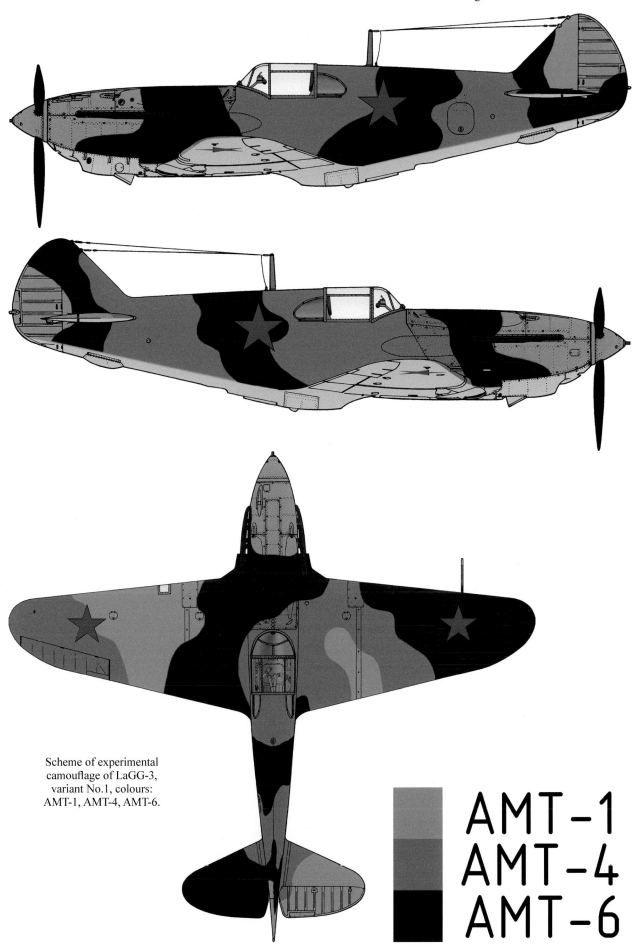

Scheme of experimental
camouflage of LaGG-3,
variant No.1, colours:
AMT-1, AMT-4, AMT-6.

AMT-1
AMT-4
AMT-6

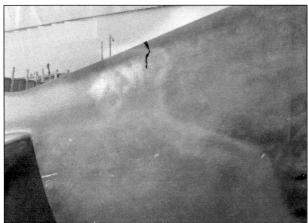

The only one photographed 'three-colour' LaGG-3, s/n 3121376. The plane got into an incident and was subsequently transferred as a training aid to the 2nd Reserve Aviation Regiment (ZAP, *Zapasnoy Aviatsionniy Polk*). Note that despite the fact that the plane had been painted with glossy aircraft lacquer, it does not look glossy on the photo.

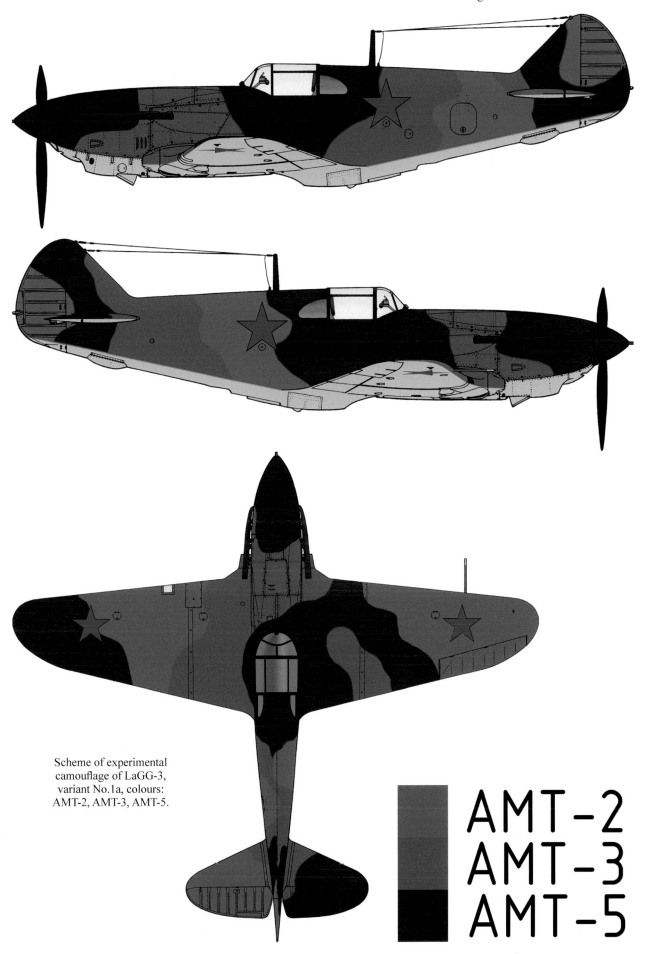

Scheme of experimental
camouflage of LaGG-3,
variant No.1a, colours:
AMT-2, AMT-3, AMT-5.

AMT-2
AMT-3
AMT-5

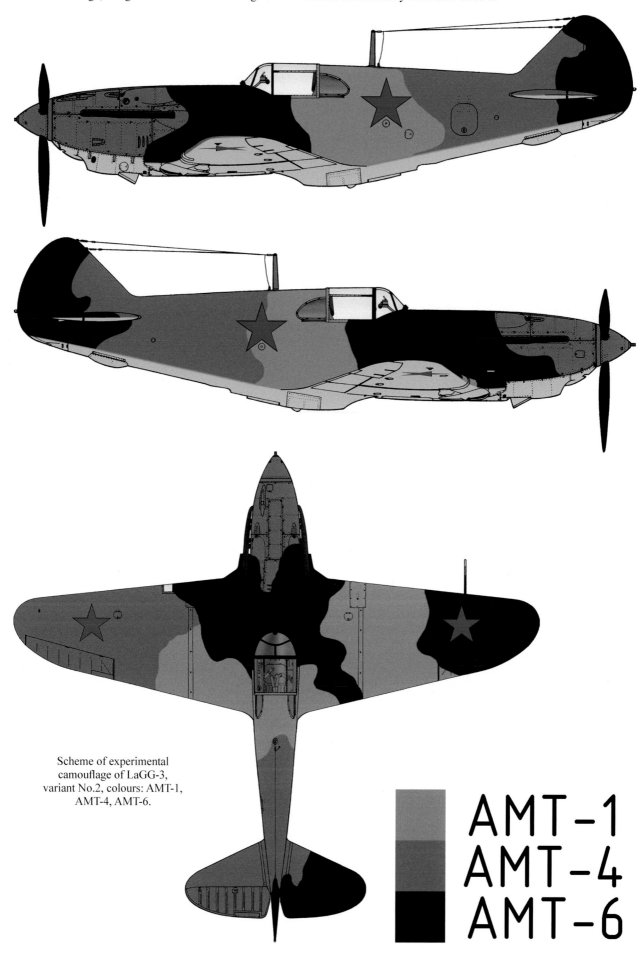

Scheme of experimental
camouflage of LaGG-3,
variant No.2, colours: AMT-1,
AMT-4, AMT-6.

AMT-1
AMT-4
AMT-6

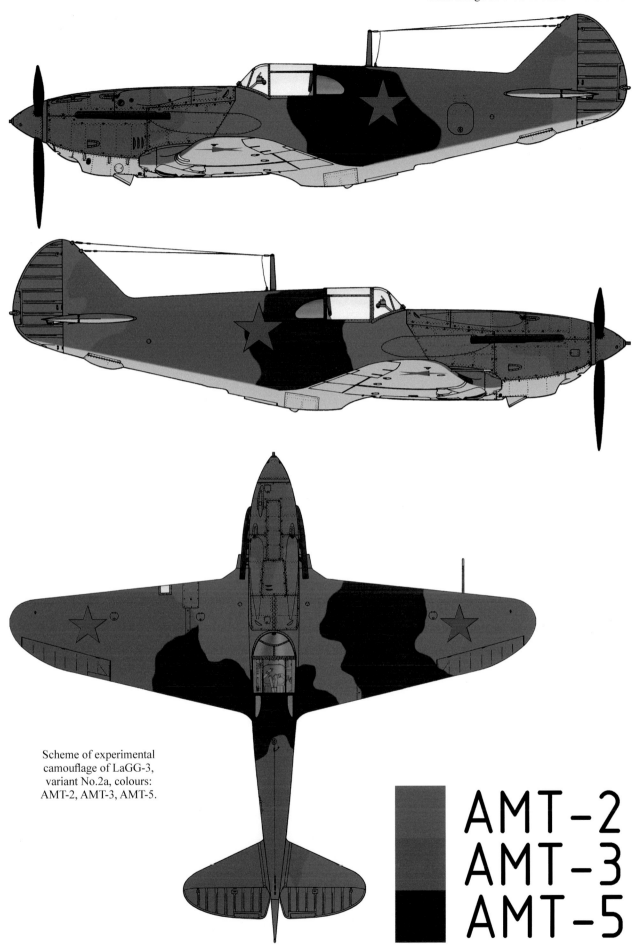

Scheme of experimental
camouflage of LaGG-3,
variant No.2a, colours:
AMT-2, AMT-3, AMT-5.

AMT-2
AMT-3
AMT-5

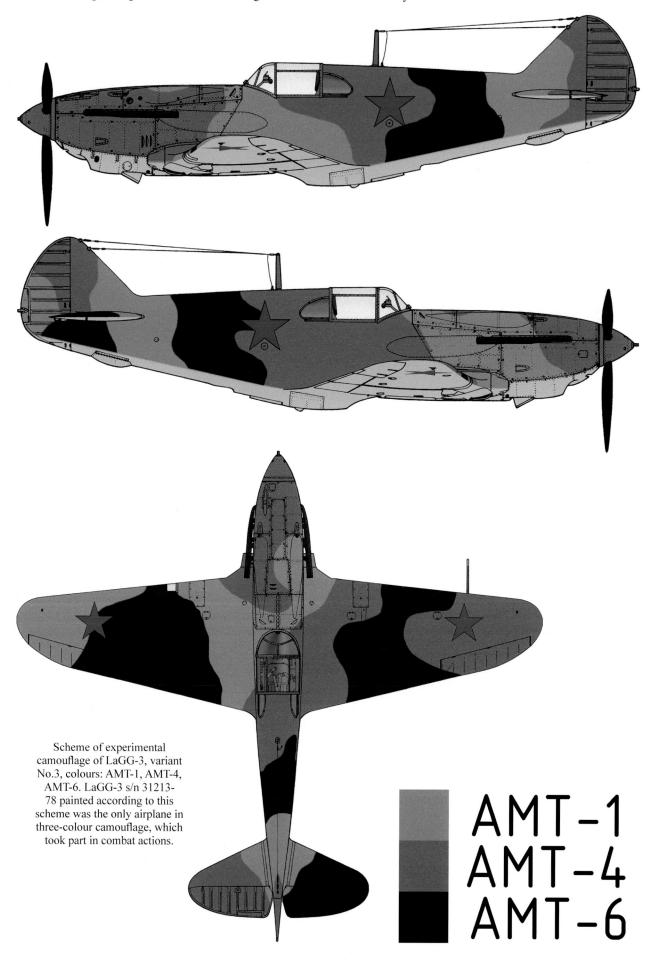

Scheme of experimental camouflage of LaGG-3, variant No.3, colours: AMT-1, AMT-4, AMT-6. LaGG-3 s/n 31213-78 painted according to this scheme was the only airplane in three-colour camouflage, which took part in combat actions.

AMT-1
AMT-4
AMT-6

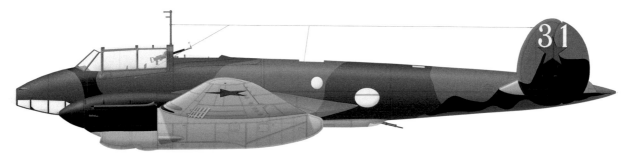

Pe-2 of the 5th SBAP, summer 1941.

Pe-2 of the 5th SBAP near Odessa, summer 1941. The airplane was manufactured after 20 June 1941, painted in experimental three-colour camouflage with insignia applied in four positions – on the wing undersides and on the vertical tail.

Pe-2 of the 40th Bomber Aviation Regiment (BAP, *Bombardirovochniy Aviatsionniy Polk*) of the Black Sea Fleet Air Force, summer 1941. The airplane was built after 20 June 1941, painted in experimental three-colour camouflage with insignia applied in four positions – on the wing undersides and on the vertical tail.

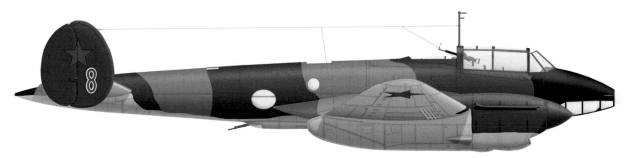

Pe-2 of an unknown unit, summer 1941.

Pe-2s of an unknown unit, pictured by the enemy at forced landing locations, summer 1941. The aircraft were painted in experimental three-colour camouflage with insignia applied in four positions – on the wing undersides and on the vertical tail.

The empennage of Pe-2 of the 410th Special-Purpose BAP, which was destroyed in July 1941 in Vitebsk; note carefully applied camouflage with straight edges.

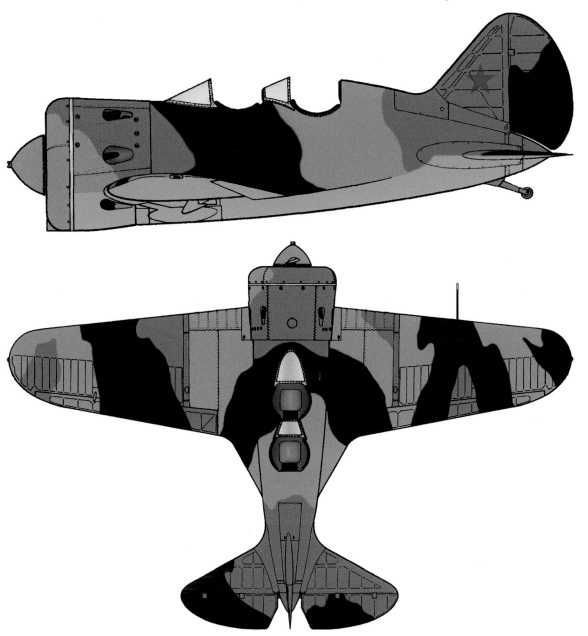

Three-colour paint scheme of the UTI-4 manufactured by Factory No.153; presumable colours – green ('protective' AII), sandy (tobacco AII), black (AII black, either MV-109 or MV-6).

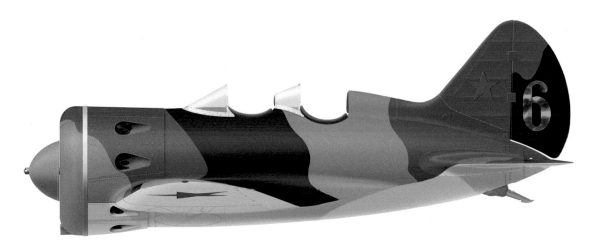

UTI-4 of 167th ZAP.

Incident with two UTI-4s s/ns 15153346 and 15153348 (manufactured by the Factory No.153 on 2 July 1941) of the 167th ZAP. The airplanes were painted in three-colour camouflage.

UTI-26-I during factory tests on 23–25 July 1940. Yak-7 (UTI-26) became the first serial aircraft of the VVS RKKA painted in two-colour black-and-green camouflage.

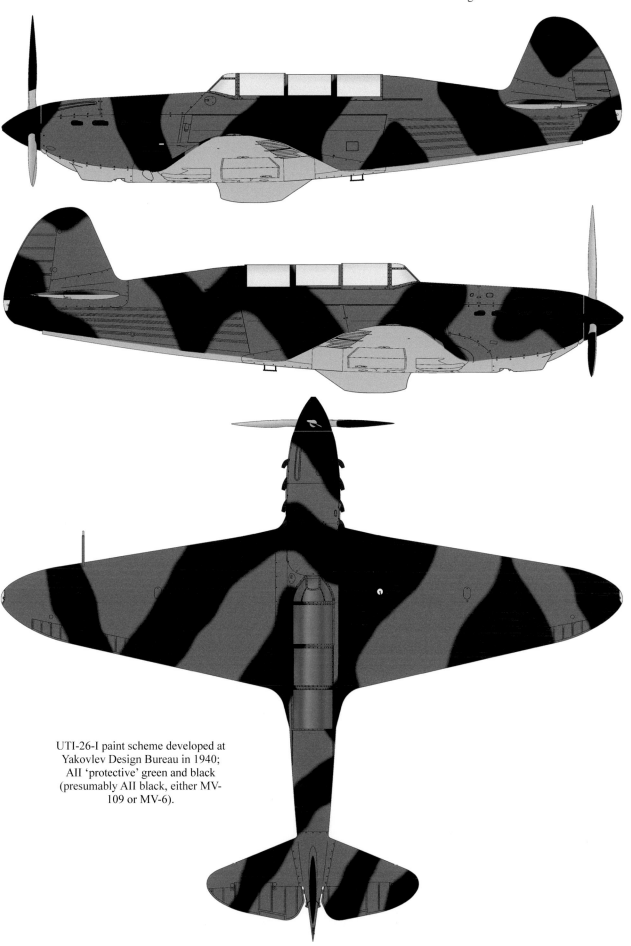

UTI-26-I paint scheme developed at Yakovlev Design Bureau in 1940; AII 'protective' green and black (presumably AII black, either MV-109 or MV-6).

UTI-26-I during factory tests on 23–25 July 1940. Yak-7
(UTI-26) became the first serial aircraft of the VVS RKKA
painted in two-colour black-and-green camouflage.

UTI-26 in the Air Force unit, winter 1941–1942; the airplane was
painted in two-colour black-and-green camouflage, similar to the
camouflage of the prototype.

A prototype of I-28 fighter in characteristic experimental camouflage during factory testing, 1940.

A prototype of I-30 fighter (the first and second prototypes) in characteristic experimental camouflage during factory testing, 1940–1941.

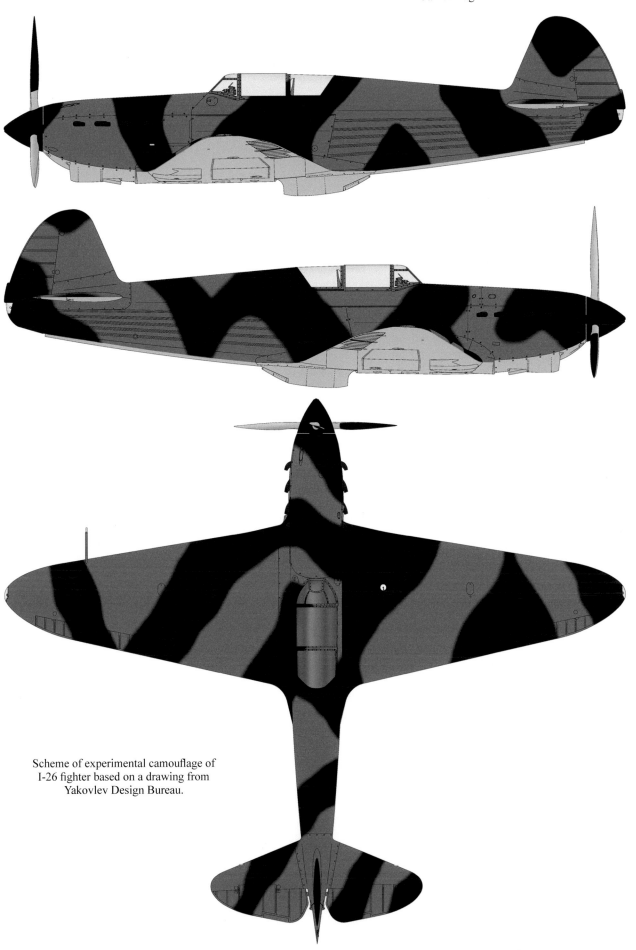

Scheme of experimental camouflage of
I-26 fighter based on a drawing from
Yakovlev Design Bureau.

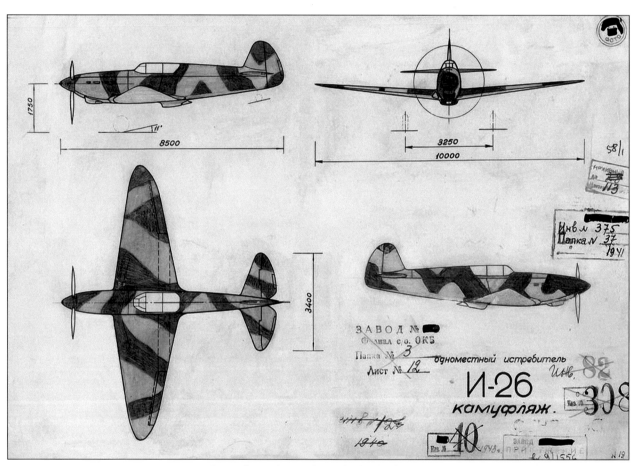

Camouflage scheme of I-26 single-seat fighter.

1

ЛАГГ-3

вариант №1

Camouflage scheme of LaGG-3 fighter. Variant No.1.

2.

ЛАГГ-3

вариант №2

Camouflage scheme of LaGG-3 fighter. Variant No.2.

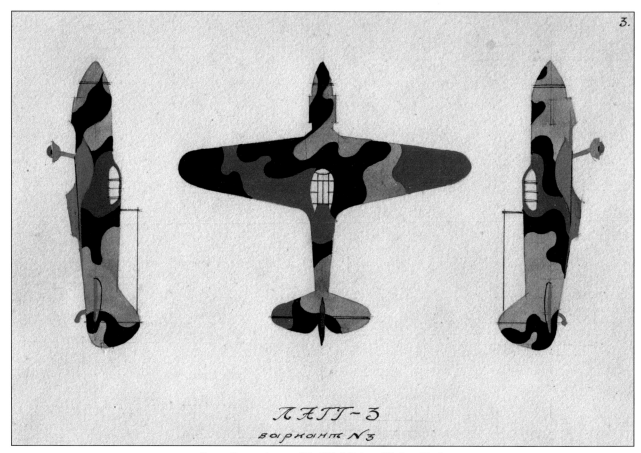

Camouflage scheme of LaGG-3 fighter. Variant No.3.

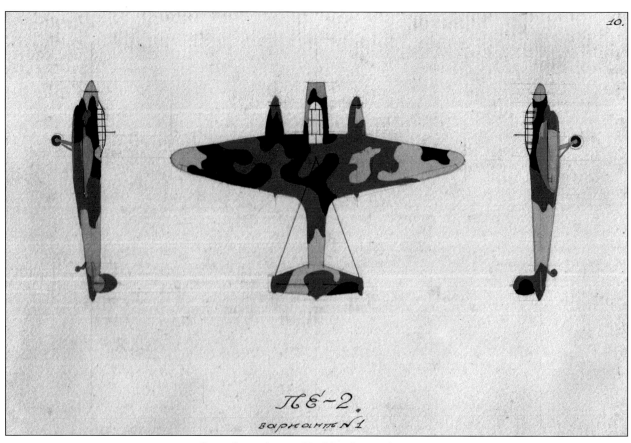

Camouflage scheme of Pe-2 bomber. Variant No.1.

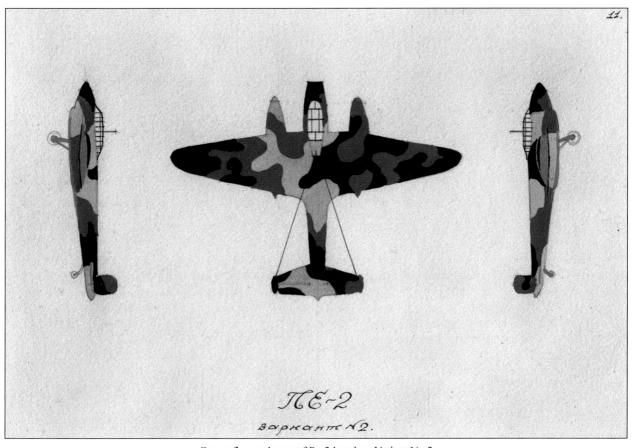

Camouflage scheme of Pe-2 bomber. Variant No.2.

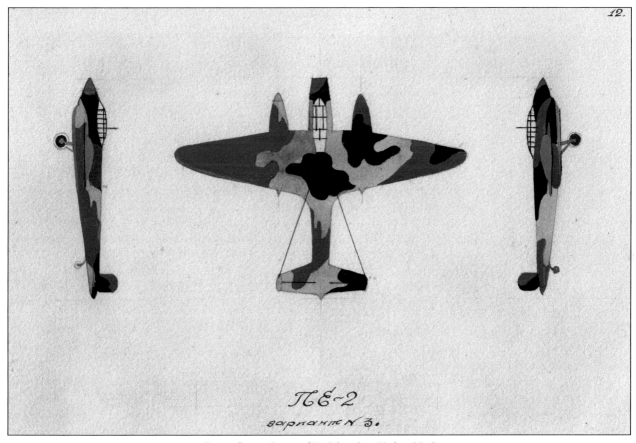

Camouflage scheme of Pe-2 bomber. Variant No.3.

2

Aircraft Factory Painting – The First Official Camouflage Scheme and the First Impromptu Camouflages

In the previous chapter it was mentioned that since 29 April 1941 and until 1 October of the same year, the preparation works were being done to switch all aircraft factories to the production of airplanes painted in a three-colour camouflage of the upper and side surfaces. Factories Nos.21 and 22 were instructed to paint 50 LaGG-3 and Pe-2 airplanes each into experimental schemes of three-colour camouflage. And since 15 July 1941 all airplanes manufactured by the aircraft factories were to be painted using matte green AMT-4 and AM-24 paints.

However, the projected work was interrupted literally in the heat of the moment. On 19 June 1941 the NKO issued Order No.0042 concerning camouflage in the Red Army. The document refers the following with regard to the VVS RKKA:

No substantial efforts have yet been taken on the camouflage of airfields and the most important military facilities.
The airfields are not all planted with grass, the runways are not painted to match the colour of the terrain, and airfield buildings with their bright colours stand out attracting the attention of observers at the distance of many kilometers.
The crowded and linear positioning of aircraft at airfields with no camouflaging and poorly organized airfield service using de-masking signs and signals expose the airfields completely.
A modern airfield must blend in completely with its surroundings, and nothing on the airfield should attract attention from the air...' (1)

The next day the SNK Directive No.1711 'On camouflage painting of airplanes, runways, tents and airfield facilities' was signed, as well as several attachments to it, including Attachments No.1 (NKAP Order No.457) and No.2 (NKO Order No.0043) (2). The Directive stated:

'In connection with the fact that already produced airplanes and those still in the process of production by the industry do not meet the modern requirements of camouflage, the Council of People's Commissars of the USSR and the Central Committee of the VKP(b) [All-Union Communist Party (Bolsheviks) – Translator's note] *have decided:*

1. *To accept the proposals of the Head of the Air Force Main Directorate, Comrade Zhigarev, and the Head of the NII VVS, Comrade Petrov, on the summer camouflage scheme of airplanes.*
2. *To require that the People's Commissariat of the Aviation Industry (Comrade Shakhurin) begin using the camouflage painting on all types of combat, training and passenger airplanes starting from 1 July 1941, in accordance with Paragraph 1 of this Directive.*
3. *To approve the NKAP order on the camouflage painting of airplanes (see Attachment 1).*
4. *To oblige the Head of the Air Force Main Directorate, Comrade Zhigarev, to arrange the following:*
    a) *by 20 July 1941 to paint all aircraft in service with camouflage paint, according to Paragraph 1 of this Directive, except for the lower surfaces, which are to retain the original painting;*
    b) *by 20 July 1941, to camouflage the runways;*
    c) *by 1 July 1941, to camouflage the tents;*
    d) *to camouflage the airfield facilities by 30 July 1941.*
5. *To approve the NKO Order 'On camouflage painting of airplanes and camouflage of runways, tents and airfield facilities in the units of Air Force' (see Attachment No.2).*
6. *To oblige the People's Commissariat of Chemical Industry (Comrade Denisov) to supply paint for the People's Commissariat of Aircraft Industry starting from 25 June 1941 in the terms, quantities and nomenclature according to Attachment No.3 and for the Air Force according to Attachments Nos.4 and 5.*

7. To approve the measures on arranging the production of camouflaging paints (see Attachment No.6).

8. To have the Air Force (Comrades Zhigarev and Petrov) submit proposals for winter camouflage painting of airplanes by 15 July 1941.

9. To oblige the NKVD [People's Commissariat of Internal Affairs – Translator's note] *(Comrade Beria) to camouflage the runways, taxiways, and aircraft parking areas by painting them for matching the background of the surrounding terrain.*

> *To oblige the Head of Air Force Zhigarev to submit to the NKVD technical specifications for camouflaging the runways, taxiways and parking areas by 10 July 1941.*

> *To oblige the State Planning Committee (Comrade Saburov), NKVD (Comrade Beria) and People's Commissariat of Chemical Industry (Comrade Denisov) to allocate the materials and means necessary to carry out the works specified in this paragraph and submit their proposals for approval by the USSR SNK.*

NKAP Order No.547 *'On camouflage colouring of manufactured airplanes'*, stated:
In order to provide camouflage colouring of produced airplanes I order the following:

1. *Directors of aircraft-building factories are supposed to switch to a matte camouflage paint scheme for the manufactured combat, training and passenger airplanes and propellers since 1 July this year in accordance with the scheme approved by the Head of Air Force, Comrade Zhigarev, and by the Head of the NII VVS, Comrade Petrov (the camouflage scheme is attached).*
2. *The camouflage painting of airplanes and propellers at Factories Nos.153 and 126 is to be implemented starting from 15 July this year.*
3. *Deputy People's Commissar, Comrade Khrunichev and Head of Main Supply Department, Comrade Sandler are to ensure an uninterrupted and regular supply of matte paint for the aircraft factories in the following quantities for the second half of the year with deliveries beginning not later than 26 June 1941:*
   (a) *blue paints: aerolacs 190 tons (including 45 tons in July); enamel paints 150 tons (including 35 tons in July);*
   b) *green paints: aerolacs 150 tons (including 35 tons in July); enamel 90 tons (including 35 tons in July);*
   c) *black paints: aerolacs 50 tons (including 15 tons in July); enamel paints 50 tons (including 10 tons in July).*
4. *Head of the First Main Directorate, Comrade Repin, and Head of the Tenth Main Directorate, Comrade Tarasovich, are supposed to provide instructions to Air Force units concerning repainting of airplanes in the units of the VVS RKKA.'*

Some shortcomings and necessary actions were indicated in the NKO Order No.0043:
'The camouflaging of the airplanes deployed in Air Force units, as well as of the runways, tents, and airfield facilities do not meet the requirements of modern camouflage standards.

This attitude toward camouflage, as one of the main types of combat readiness of Air Force, cannot be tolerated any further.

Thereby I order:

1. *By 20 July 1941, using the strength of the Air Force units with involvement of personnel of the aircraft repair workshops, to complete the camouflage painting of all available airplanes according to the attached painting scheme, except for the undersides, which should retain the original paint...*

> *Commanders of the Air Force districts are to report on the progress of the airplane camouflaging works to the Head of the VVS RKKA Main Directorate from 9 p.m. to 11 p.m. daily using high-frequency communication.*

In accordance with these documents, the camouflage schemes were sent to Air Force units and NKAP factories. In fact, it was one scheme with two-colour camouflage that used green and black paints. The paints chosen were AMT-4 green nitro paint for wooden or percale surfaces and AM-24 oil enamel for metal surfaces. Correspondingly, the black AMT-6 was chosen for wooden or percale surfaces and AM-26 for metal. The propeller was supposed to be painted a black with AM-26 oil paint. Insignia were now supposed to be applied in four positions, on the wing undersides and on the vertical tail.

Judging by the approved scheme, the camouflage scheme was based on the paint scheme used for prototypes of the Yakovlev Design Bureau at the Factory No.115. It was a little modified, and according to some reports, proposed by the new Head of the NII VVS, General I.F. Petrov. However, there is no doubt that they used the ideas of the Yakovlev Design Bureau; in fact, even the aircraft types pictured on the scheme look like Yakovlev I-26 fighter and BB-22 bomber. This was indirectly confirmed by Yakovlev himself in his book 'The Purpose of Life':

Stalin took a detailed interest in the ways of camouflaging airplanes abroad. When he learnt that the Germans, as well as Americans and British covered their planes with three-colour camouflage to match the surrounding terrain, he reproached us for being careless. During the meeting it turned out that one of the institutes of the People's Commissariat of Defense, which was developing camouflage designs, had several options for aircraft camouflage painting, but had not yet issued a final solution. We were called irresponsible bureaucrats and given three days to offer suggestions for aircraft camouflage.

Within the specified time frame, our design bureau produced models of various types of aircraft with camouflage paint.

After discussing the issue with the People's Commissar of the Aviation Industry and representatives of the Air Force we showed these models in the Kremlin. The models were approved, and the leaders of the Air Force were charged with the duty to camouflage all aircraft within the shortest time possible.' (3)

According to the records of the Stalin's office visitors, Head of the Air Force Main Directorate Lieutenant General of Aviation P.F. Zhigarev, Head of NII VVS Major General of Aviation I.F. Petrov, People's Commissar of the Aviation Industry A.I. Shakhurin and his deputy in charge of experimental aircraft construction A.S. Yakovlev visited the leader of the Soviet Union on 17–18 June 1941. It is obvious that on one of these days the issue of the urgent introduction of airplane camouflage painting was scrutinized, and it was decided to accept two-colour camouflage for the VVS RKKA, based on the camouflage of prototypes of the Yakovlev Design Bureau. Doing anything otherwise was simply unfeasible within three days, and the question whether the approved colour scheme was optimal or not remains debatable.

It was clearly impossible to immediately switch to the chosen camouflage schemes at the aircraft factories and Air Force units, primarily due to the lack of the very paints as well as approved copies of the schemes that had yet to be produced and delivered to factories and regiments.

Besides, the further course of events was obviously greatly influenced by several factors: the main one was the perfidious attack of Nazi Germany on the USSR on 22 June 1941; another important factor was the failure of nearly all NKAP enterprises to fulfill the plan of aircraft production in the first half of 1941. After the beginning of the war, it was of paramount importance to increase the production rate, so many tasks were carried out rather formally, and there are almost no detailed records about actions undertaken to introduce camouflage painting of aircraft at most of the factories. Factory No.21 is an exception.

According to the joint act of the Factory No.21 and VIAM on painting 50 LaGG-3 fighters into experimental camouflages it is known that the instructions to paint the airplanes into black-and-green camouflage were received as early as on 22 June 1941. Moreover, it was ordered to cover the aircraft with paints AMT-4 and AMT-6. (4)

The first six LaGG-3s were painted into black-and-green camouflage according to a temporary scheme as early as on 23 June; apparently, there was no time to sketch the template of this camouflage scheme, so it is not known how it looked. Then, on 24 June two schemes were approved jointly by the Director of Factory No.21 and a representative of VIAM. One of these schemes survived and is a camouflage of large patches of black and green paints, which is very different from the typical camouflage. It is very likely that the black-and-green camouflage paint scheme was applied on the first airplanes of the 4th series. Unfortunately, the number of aircraft painted at Factory No.21 under temporary schemes Nos.4 and 5 is not indicated in the documents. (5)

On 1 July 1941 a train with 15 LaGG-3s left to the 147th IAP, with the destination of Kola railway station. On the spot the airplanes were not handed over to 147th IAP but instead to the neighboring 145th IAP. Among the delivered airplanes there was LaGG-3 s/n 31214-6, which later was flown by Captain L.A. Galchenko, Squadron Commander of the 145th IAP. This airplane was very remarkable for a few reasons: it was the sixth LaGG-3 which had an armament composing of one ShVAK cannon, one BS and two ShKAS machine guns, then it was accepted by the military acceptance between 22 and 27 June and, judging by the photo, was painted into one of the temporary schemes of the black-and-green camouflage. It is confirmed both by presence of black-and-green spots (unfortunately, the photos of 1942 fail show what variant, No.4 or No.5, was used), and by the fact that the stars were applied in four positions: on the wing undersides and on the vertical tail, that is, according to the scheme approved on 20 June 1941. The assumption that the aircraft were painted in black-and-green camouflage starting from the airplanes of the 4th series is also indirectly confirmed by the fact that out of the 15 LaGG-3s which arrived in the Arctic region, 12 were of the 3rd series, and three – s/ns 31214-5, 31214-6 and 31214-10, belonged to the 4th series. Judging by the photos from the accident reports and the photos of downed LaGG-3s taken by German servicemen, the airplanes of the 3rd series which were released from the factory in mid-June were not camouflaged, unlike the airplane s/n 31214-6.

Painting airplanes in accordance with the scheme, approved by the SNK Directive No.1711 of 20 June 1941, was started at Factory No.21 most likely at the end of June. Unfortunately, the documents did not record exact date and serial number of the airplane which was the first to receive this camouflage. At the end of June and in the first two decades of July the factory was feverishly eliminating numerous design and manufacturing defects in LaGG-3s. Regular deliveries of airplanes to the Air Force units began only on 22 July. For this reason, the photos of airplanes which were painted and received insignia according to the approved scheme have not been discovered yet. Judging by the photos taken during tests, Factory No.21 continued to paint the airplanes, starting with the temporary black-and-green camouflage schemes, by applying the reversing camouflage colours on every other airplane. (6)

At the time when the factory in Gorky was already painting the airplanes into experimental three-colour camouflages, Factory No.22 was still mastering the process. In Moscow the aircraft manufacturer started applying camouflages on the Pe-2 a little later. Probably it was caused by the untimely delivery of new oil paints. According to the documents of the factory, oil paints AM-21/22/23/24/25/26 were received only on 14 June, and as of 18 June 1941, 15 wing center sections and ten fuselage nose parts were prepared for painting. The actual process of painting the camouflage was supposed to start only on 24 June with the first airplane of the 21st series (Pe-2 s/n 1/21). Despite the SNK Directive No.1711 and the beginning of the war, many photos of the Pe-2s show that the previous order to paint 50 bombers in three-colour camouflages was fulfilled. Considering the fact that the military acceptance report for June says that Factory No.22 delivered 71 camouflaged airplanes, apparently the factory switched to black-and-green scheme immediately after completing the painting in three-colour camouflages. In July, according to the report of the military representative, all the accepted airplanes were camouflaged. It is yet unknown how the airplanes were painted – according to the approved scheme, or it was done according to some temporary scheme at first. (7)

Judging by photos from tests of airplanes s/ns 16/32, 5/33 and 10/35, as well as by Soviet newsreels, the Pe-2s produced by Factory No.22 were painted in standard camouflage, according to the approved scheme. However, due to the fact the factory was only priming the aircraft, while the actual painting was done at Moscow Central airfield, the very painting of camouflage spots, though in general conformed to the approved scheme, was usually very 'loose' and was done carelessly with some deviations from airplane to airplane.

By the present time, basing on the review of available photos and newsreels, only airplanes of the 28th–31st series have been identified, which carry standard black-and-green camouflage, with stars in four positions, but already of enlarged size (implemented starting from Pe-2 s/n 6/28). Photos of airplanes of the 21st–27th series of the proper quality, with black-and-green camouflage and small-sized stars in four positions, have not been found yet. (8)

Another enterprise that was building Pe-2s, Kazan Aircraft Factory No.124, also painted the first series of these airplanes, produced in early July 1941, in accordance with the approved black-and-green scheme, with the stars in four positions. Unfortunately, it is not known which paint was used at the factory. (9)

An interesting version of camouflage was found on the Pe-2s built at Moscow Factory No.39. The airplanes received very specific black spots, shaped as a thin curly line. The camouflage was not applied in Air Force units, which is confirmed by the fact that similar schemes are known on the aircraft of different regiments that operated in different parts of the front. At that, the airplanes belonged to different production series and carried insignia that varied in different periods. Most likely the camouflage was applied on Pe-2s of 11th–12th series manufactured at the end of June 1941, as the airplanes of the 12th series were delivered to the 5th SBAP of the South Front Air Force at the beginning of June, which were later pictured by German photographers in course of invasion. Moreover, there exists an accident report of the Pe-2 s/n 390515 from the 50th SBAP. This airplane of the 5th series produced by Factory No.39 in spring 1941 was passed to the training regiment of the Air Force Academy, but after the accident it was repaired at the factory and apparently received an improvised black-and-green camouflage and stars in four positions, the same as on the airplanes of the 11th–12th series. In addition, the same camouflage was also applied on the airplanes at the end of July. It was also noted on the Pe-2s of the late series, up to and including the 17th, which already had a new scheme of insignia application. There is no information, however, on the types of paints used. (10)

Another aircraft type which began to get the camouflage according to the approved scheme was the Il-2 produced at Factory No.18. No documents have been found which detail the manufacturing processes in Voronezh, but numerous photos clearly indicate the use of the camouflage according to the scheme attached to the SNK Directive No.1711 for painting the production Il-2s. However, at this time it is impossible to determine where exactly the airplanes were painted – at the factory or at the 1st Reserve Aviation Brigade, although almost all new ground attack airplanes passed. It is also unknown what paint types were used to camouflage the airplanes. The black spots were most likely applied with a brush. Interestingly, after a while, probably in August, the Il-2s were painted with significant deviations from the approved scheme, so there is a possibility that the camouflage painting was performed in the 1st Reserve Aviation Brigade.

There are photos of several downed and damaged Il-2 airplanes taken by Wehrmacht soldiers that clearly belonged to the 61st and 74th ShAP, which received the airplanes in the first decade of July 1941. Moreover, there are photos of several airplanes (place and time unknown) painted according to the scheme attached to the SNK Directive No.1711 in black-and-green camouflage, with stars placed in four positions (wing undersides and vertical tail), photographed by German soldiers at the sites of forced landings. These Il-2s most likely belonged to the 61st, 74th, 232nd and 430th ShAP, because those units received the Il-2 produced at the end of June – beginning of July 1941.

One of the paradoxes in the history of implementing the approved camouflage scheme involved the situation with the Yak-1 airplanes produced at Factory No.292. It might seem that the standard scheme was the brainchild of the Yakovlev Design Bureau, and, in fact, was drawn on the general views of its first fighter, but Factory No.292, which produced the first Yak, was not among the leaders of the 'camouflaging' process. There were objective reasons for this. Firstly, the factory did not have a proper workshop for painting airplanes, and secondly, there was insufficient number of spray guns available. Therefore, only metal parts were painted with oil paint using spray gun, while wooden and percale surfaces were painted with nitro lacquers using a brush. Since the process of painting took place in a dusty hangar, it turned the outer skin surface into almost 'sandpaper', according to the report of the military representative of the factory. As result, this defect negatively affected the aerodynamics of the new fighters. According to the data of military acceptance, the speed of the camouflaged airplanes decreased by 12–16 km/h. Despite such difficulties, the factory began to paint the airplanes in late June – early July in black-and-green camouflage, but with serious deviations from the approved scheme. Moreover, painting according to the temporary scheme continued at least until early August. The used paints were green (AII 'protective' green nitro lacquer) and black (AII black nitro lacquer); the stars were placed in four positions according to the SNK Directive No.1711. (11)

The Su-2 airplanes manufactured at Factory No.135 also received black-and-green camouflage, but so far no information has been found about the starting date of the camouflage application, as well as on schemes and paint types used. The July report of military representative says only that the new airplanes were camouflaged. Judging by the photos taken by German servicemen, the Su-2s were painted at Factory No.135 with significant deviations from the standard scheme. A distinguishing feature of the airplanes produced by this factory was a small star insignia, applied on the rudder in a specific location. It is somewhat likely that the Su-2s built at Factory No.207 were painted in accordance with the scheme attached to the SNK Directive No.1711. However, due to the insignificant volume of the airplanes produced (eight aircraft were delivered by the factory in Dolgoprudny in July and 12 in August), it is almost impossible to get an idea of how their painting looked like. (12)

An ideal example of the airplane, perfectly painted in the black-and-green camouflage in accordance with SNK Directive No.1711, with stars in four positions, can be seen in the photos from the test reports of the Su-2 in the artillery spotter version. This Su-2 is from the early series, production of which ended in May–June 1941. Most likely, the airplane was repainted in the process of its modification at Factory No.289 (13). There is a probability that Factory No.289 rolled out series production Su-2s also in black-and-green camouflage, painted in accordance with the approved scheme and with stars of enlarged size. There exists a photo of one such aircraft after a forced landing.

There is some probability that two other enterprises painted their airplanes in black-and-green camouflage. These are Factories Nos.23 and 81. By 22 June 1941 at the Factory No.81 there were 36 Yak-4 reconnaissance airplanes. It is possible that before delivery to Air Force units these aircraft (in July, the 314th and 316th RAPs received 18 airplanes each) were painted in black-and-green standard camouflage with insignia in four positions. It is unknown what paint types were used in the process.

Factory No.23 in June–July 1941 manufactured 65 LaGG-3 fighters (30 were delivered in July, with 25 of them went to the 19th IAP and another five to the Red-Banner Baltic Fleet Air Force; the rest were sent to the 44th and 157th IAPs in August), some of which, before they were delivered to the regiments, could have been painted in improvised black-and-green camouflage with insignia applied in four positions. This is partly confirmed by photos of the 44th IAP airplanes taken in August–September 1941.

The story with the introduction of new camouflages at Factory No.1 stands apart. The new MiG-3 fighters did not receive the approved black-and-green camouflage. For a while they were rolled out from the factory in overall green paint on the upper surfaces, but with stars in four positions. The author has not found a document explaining this situation. Presumably this was caused by the extensive work carried out by the factory in June related to the modification of control surfaces on 250 airplanes that had been completely assembled by then. Most likely, painting of airplanes in black-and-green camouflage was considered an excessive load and was limited to the application of insignia in approved positions. It is indirectly confirmed by the painting and placing insignia on 19 I-153 fighters which were being overhauled at the same time at the factory in early July, and later were transferred to the 160th IAP. In 6–7 July 1941 these airplanes were filmed at the airfield in Smolensk. It is not known exactly what paint types were used to cover the aircraft, but most likely it was the same AII 'protective' green nitro lacquer of the second coating.

Summing up this chapter, it should be noted that the history of introducing the new black-and-green camouflage schemes with a new arrangement of insignia at the NKAP factories in accordance with the SNK Directive No.1711 is still under study at the moment. Given the tight deadlines for implementation of the painting scheme established by the government, difficult situation related to the failure of the majority of enterprises to meet the aircraft production schedules, and the short period of time (about 20–30 days) during which the aircraft were released from the factories in such camouflage, as well as due to the lack or insufficiency of records from many factories, it should be admitted that the full picture of events is unlikely to be ever recovered. One thing is certain – virtually all the aircraft factories complied with the SNK Directive No.1711 and the NKAP order No.547, and starting from 22–30 June 1941, switched to painting the aircraft in black-and-green camouflage with the application of insignia in four positions. In this sense it is worth noting that even Novosibirsk Factory No.153, which had been allowed to begin camouflaging airplanes starting from 15 July, managed with this task ahead of schedule and began applying new camouflage from 27 June (see Chapter 1). However, to be fair, it should also be noted that most factories failed to receive the new paint and painting schemes. At least for the month of July, the airplanes were camouflaged with old paints from the remaining stocks and according to temporary schemes. Consequently, it was then impossible to radically solve the issue of aircraft camouflage at that time. This was not the fault of the aircraft factories, as the problem was caused by the fact that the enterprises of chemical industry could not change the previous plans and instantly switch over to the production of new paints.

Factory No.1 became an outsider in executing the state orders, as for objective reasons it could not immediately repaint several hundred airplanes accumulated on its territory and managed to correct the insignia positions only. Factories Nos.22 and 21 predictably became the leaders in this process and began to paint the aircraft in new scheme on schedule since they originally were in a favorable position and had received the new paints before 20 June 1941 due to the earlier work on testing of experimental three-colour camouflages. The process of introducing new paints AMT-4/6 and AM-24/26, as well as standard black-and-green camouflage schemes at NKAP factories was far from over, and these measures were overlain by the decision to introduce the new scheme of insignia application in six positions, taken in the second half of July.

List of documents employed:
1. ЦАМО, ф.4, оп.11, д.62, л.201–203.
2. ГАРФ, ф.5446, оп. 106, д. 20, л.31. ЦАМО, ф.4, оп.11, д.62, л.204–205.
3. A.S. Yakovlev. *Tsel Zhizni*. Politizdat, Moscow, 1973. Pages 224–225.
4. ЦАМО, ф.35, оп.11287, д.83, л.268–275.
5. ЦАМО, ф.35, оп.11287, д.83, л.268–275.
6. ЦАМО, ф.35, оп.11287, д.83, л.268–275.
7. ЦАМО, ф.35, оп.11287, д.519, л.30, 192–195.
8. ЦАМО, ф.35, оп.11287, д.16, л.212–214.
9. ЦАМО, ф.35, оп.11294, д.197, л.10–20.
10. ЦАМО, ф.35, оп.11294, д.196, л.149–164.
11. ЦАМО, ф.35, оп.11605, д.5119, л.50–60.
12. ЦАМО, ф.35, оп.11287, д.214, л.161.

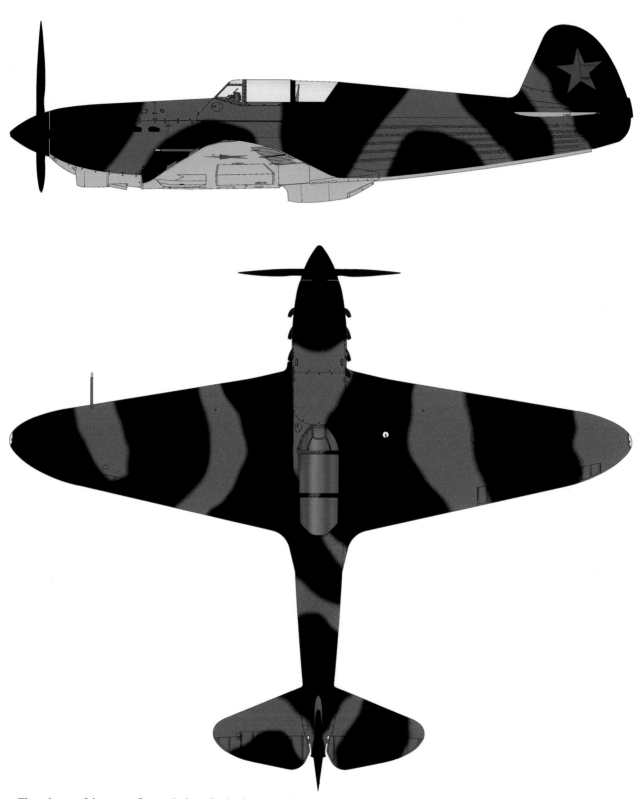

The scheme of the camouflage painting of a single-engine airplane established by SNK Directive No.1711 of 20 June 1941 for the VVS RKKA airplanes. Colour: green (paint: AMT-4 or AM-24) and black (AMT-6 or AM-26), propeller painted in black AM-26.

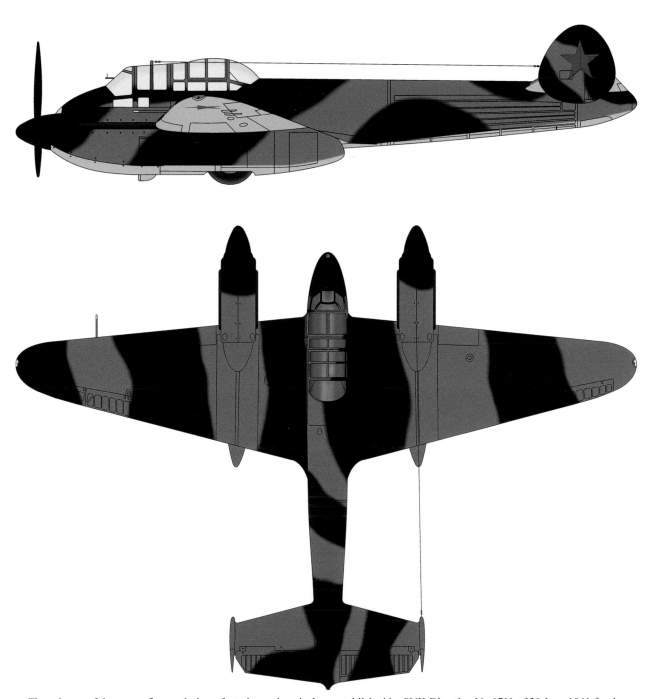

The scheme of the camouflage painting of a twin-engine airplane established by SNK Directive No.1711 of 20 June 1941 for the VVS RKKA airplanes. Colour: green (paint AMT-4 or AM-24) and black (AMT-6 or AM-26), propeller painted in black AM-26.

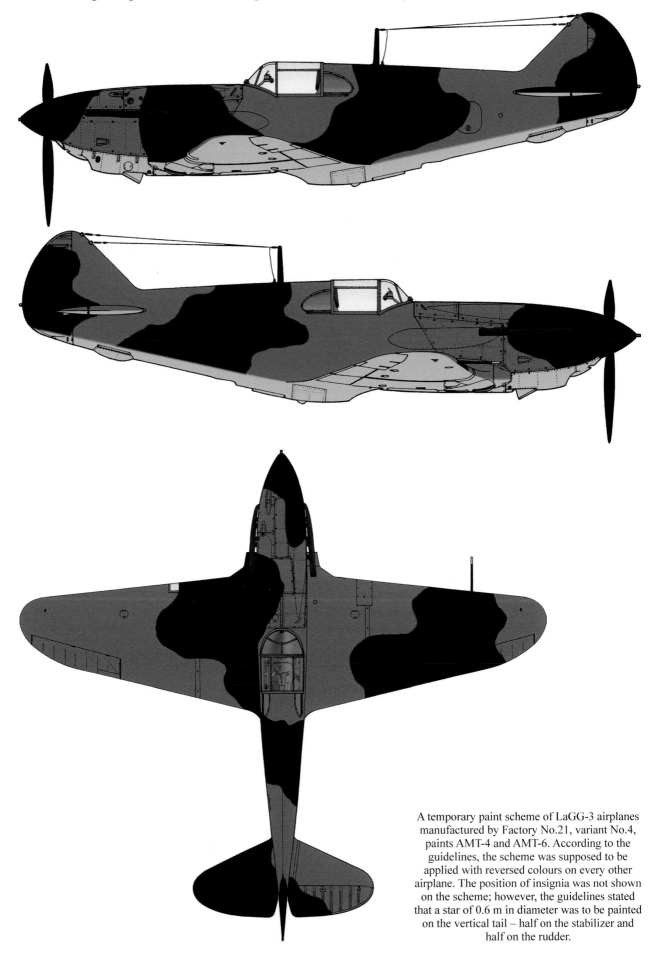

A temporary paint scheme of LaGG-3 airplanes manufactured by Factory No.21, variant No.4, paints AMT-4 and AMT-6. According to the guidelines, the scheme was supposed to be applied with reversed colours on every other airplane. The position of insignia was not shown on the scheme; however, the guidelines stated that a star of 0.6 m in diameter was to be painted on the vertical tail – half on the stabilizer and half on the rudder.

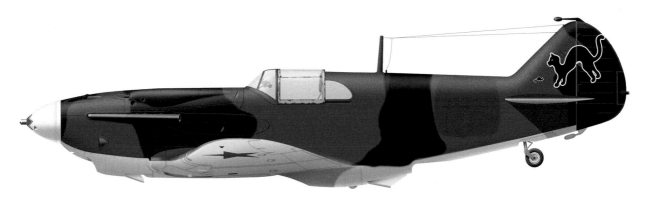

LaGG-3 s/n 31214-6 from the 145th IAP, spring–summer of 1942.

 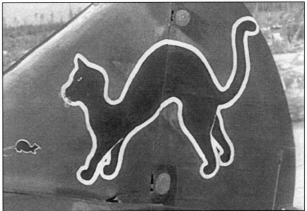

LaGG-3 s/n 31214-6 from the 145th IAP, flown by Captain L.A. Galchenko. Most likely it was painted in black-and-green temporary camouflage of Factory No.21 (variant No.4 or not standardized variant from among six LaGG-3s painted without compiling a scheme). The AMT-4 and AMT-6 paints were used on upper surfaces and light blue nitro lacquer II undersides; the propeller blades painted in AM-26 black. The insignia were applied in four positions with red nitro lacquer II. The airplane was photographed in the spring and summer of 1942.

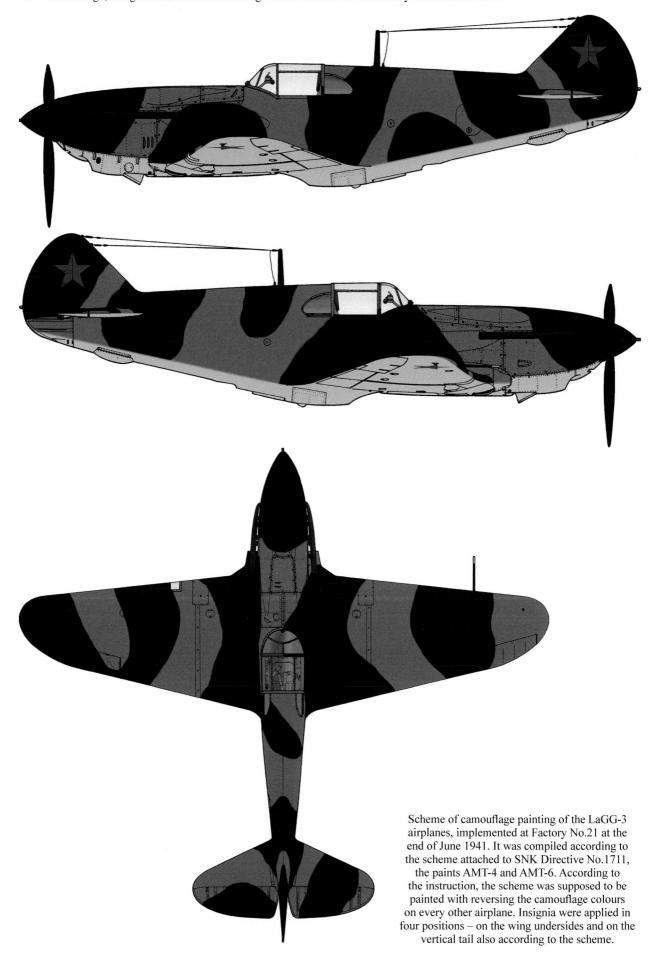

Scheme of camouflage painting of the LaGG-3 airplanes, implemented at Factory No.21 at the end of June 1941. It was compiled according to the scheme attached to SNK Directive No.1711, the paints AMT-4 and AMT-6. According to the instruction, the scheme was supposed to be painted with reversing the camouflage colours on every other airplane. Insignia were applied in four positions – on the wing undersides and on the vertical tail also according to the scheme.

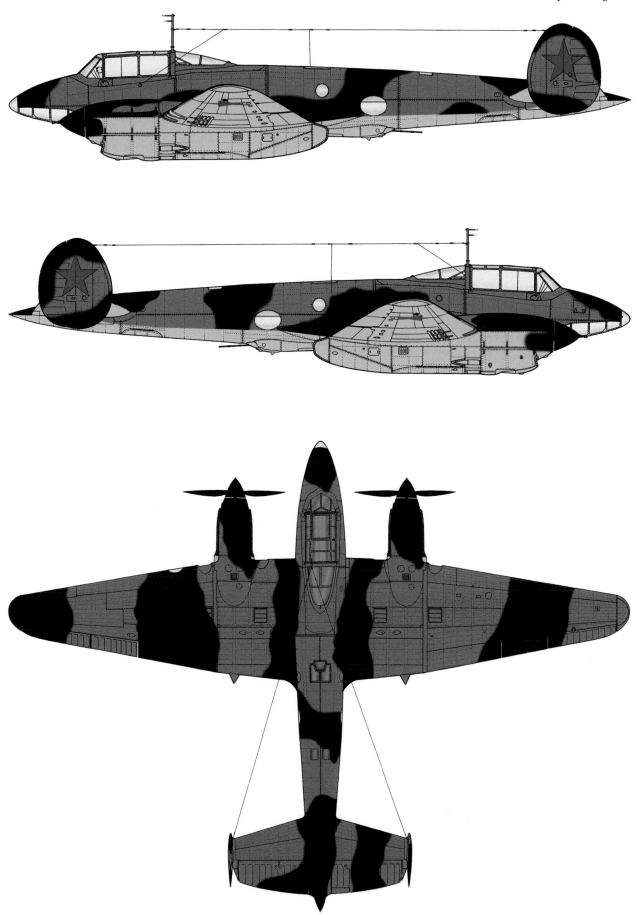

Scheme of camouflage painting of Pe-2 airplane, implemented at Factory No.22 at the end of June 1941. It was compiled according to the scheme attached to the SNK Directive No.1711, with paints AM-24 and AM-26.

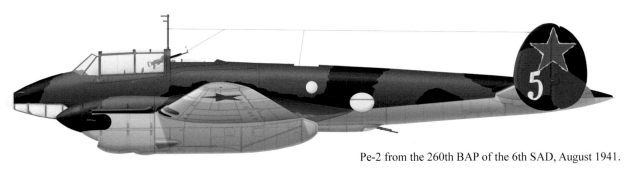

Pe-2 from the 260th BAP of the 6th SAD, August 1941.

Pe-2, tactical number '5 white' (airplane of the 29th series of Factory No.22), from the 260th BAP of the 6th Composite Aviation Division (SAD, *Smeshannaya Aviatsionnaya Diviziya*), August 1941. The airplane was painted in black-and-green camouflage, with insignia applied in four positions (on the wing undersides and on the vertical tail) according to the scheme attached to SNK Directive No.1711; the stars on the vertical fins are of enlarged size.

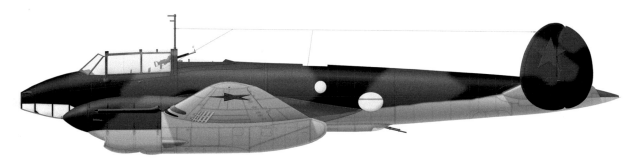

Pe-2 s/n 105, built by Factory No.124.

Pe-2 s/n 105, built by Factory No.124 (the fifth airplane of the first series), lost in an accident. The airplane was painted in black-and-green camouflage, insignia applied in four positions (wing undersides and on the vertical tail) according to the scheme attached to the SNK Directive No.1711.

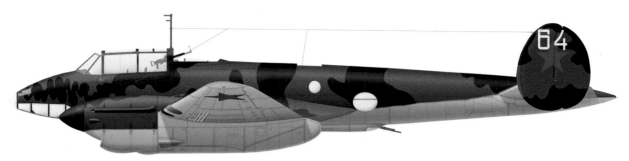

Pe-2 from the 5th SBAP of the Southern Front Air Force.

Right and below: Pe-2 presumably of the 12th series, tactical number 64, from the 5th SBAP of the Southern Front Air Force, captured at the place of forced landing. The airplane was built by Factory No.39 and painted in the improvised black-and-green camouflage, but the insignia were put in four positions – on the wing undersides and on the vertical tail according to the scheme attached to the SNK Directive No.1711.

Another Pe-2 from the 5th SBAP of the Southern Front Air Force was painted in the improvised black-and-green camouflage, with insignia applied in four positions – on the wing undersides and on the vertical tail, according to the scheme attached to the SNK Directive No.1711. The airplane was destroyed by fire after forced landing.

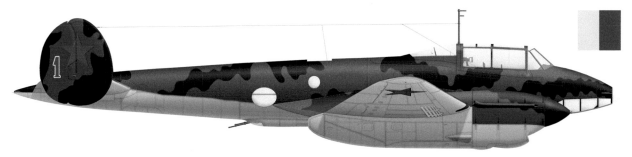

Pe-2 of the 5th series s/n 390515 from the 50th SBAP.

Crash landing of Pe-2 of the 5th series s/n 390515, tactical number 1, from the 50th SBAP. The airplane was built by Factory No.39 and painted in the improvised black-and-green camouflage. The insignia were put in four positions – on the wing undersides and on the vertical tail, according to the scheme attached to the SNK Directive No.1711.

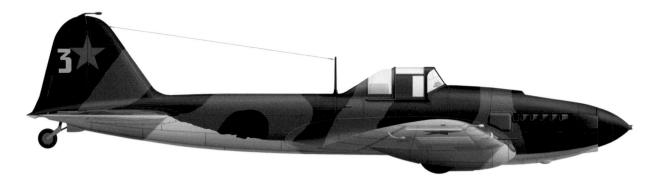

Il-2 presumably from the 61st ShAP, Shatalovo airfield.

Il-2, tactical number 3, presumably from the 61st ShAP photographed by German soldiers at Shatalovo airfield. The airplane was painted in black-and-green camouflage according to the scheme attached to SNK Directive No.1711, the insignia applied in four positions (wing undersides and vertical tail).

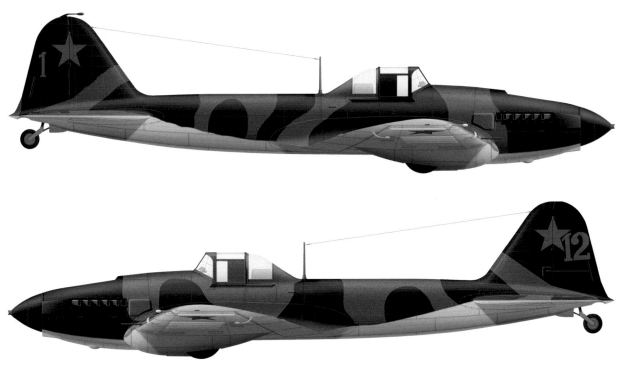

Il-2s presumably from the 61st ShAP, July 1941.

Il-2s, tactical numbers 1 and 12, presumably from the 61st ShAP, captured by the enemy at the place of forced landing in the middle of July 1941. The airplanes were painted according to the scheme attached to the SNK Directive No.1711 in black-and-green camouflage, with insignia applied in four positions (wing undersides and vertical tail).

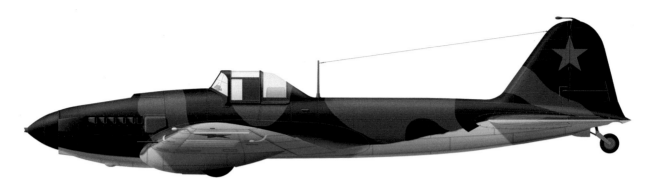

Il-2 presumably from the 74th ShAP.

Il-2s presumably from the 74th ShAP, painted in black-and-green camouflage according to the scheme attached to the SNK Directive No.1711, with insignia applied in four positions (wing undersides and vertical tail), photographed by German troops at the sites of forced landings.

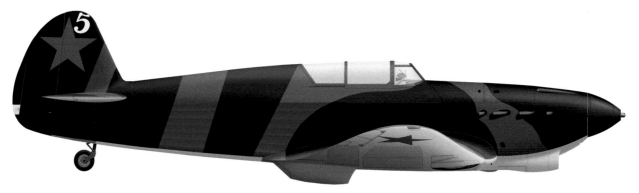

Yak-1 s/n 1411 of the 13th ZAP. The airplane was painted according to the improvised black-and-green scheme adopted by Factory No.292. The paints used – green (AII 'protective' green nitro lacquer) and black (AII black nitro lacquer), while the insignia were placed in four positions according to the SNK Directive No.1711.

Yak-1 of the 11th series s/n 1411, tactical number '5 white'. The airplane was handed over to the 13th ZAP before 12 July 1941. On 31 August 1941, the fighter flown by the pilot Junior Lieutenant G.A. Kuznetsov made a crash landing.

Yak-1 of the 21st series, airfield of Factory No.292, July 1941.

Collision of two Yak-1s of the 16th and 21st series s/ns 1816 and 1221, at the airfield of Factory No.292 on 12 July 1941. The airplanes were painted similarly to s/n 1411, in the improvised black-and-green camouflage.

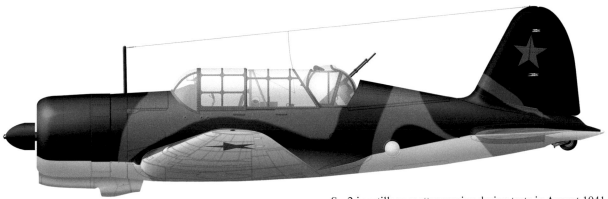

Su-2 in artillery spotter version during tests in August 1941.

Su-2 in artillery spotter version during tests in August 1941. The airplane was painted in black-and-green camouflage, insignia were applied in four positions (wing undersides and vertical tail), according to the scheme attached to the SNK Directive No.1711.

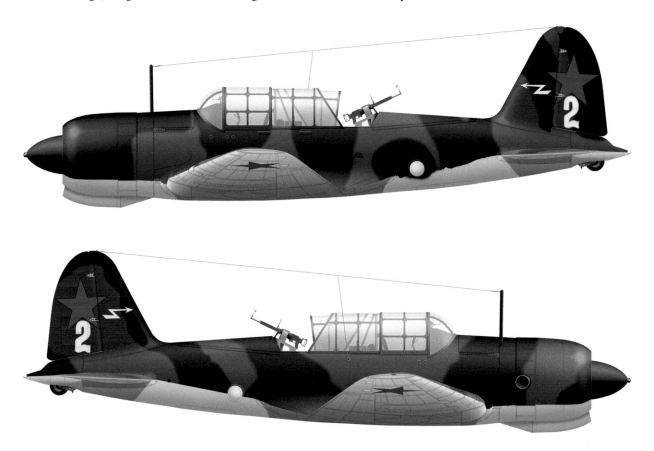

Su-2 presumably from the 226th Short-Range BAP, summer 1941.

Su-2, tactical number 2, presumably from the 226th Short-Range BAP, captured by the enemy at the place of forced landing, summer 1941. The airplane was painted in black-and-green camouflage and carried insignia in four positions according to the scheme attached to the SNK Directive No.1711. Note that the star on the rudder is already of enlarged size.

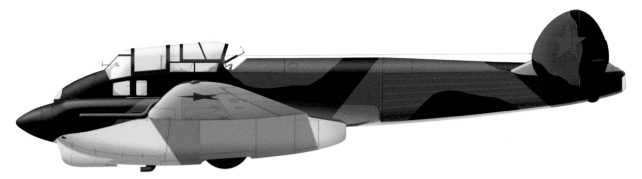

Yak-4 presumably from the 314th or 316th RAP.

Yak-4 presumably from the 314th or 316th RAP. The airplane was painted in standard black-and-green camouflage, insignia were applied in four positions (wing undersides and vertical tail), according to the scheme attached to the SNK Directive No.1711.

LaGG-3s from the 44th IAP of the 7th IAK of the Air Defense Forces.

LaGG-3s manufactured by Factory No.23, from the 44th IAP of the 7th IAK of the Air Defense Forces. The airplanes were painted in improvised black-and-green camouflage but carried insignia in four positions according to the scheme attached to the SNK Directive No.1711.

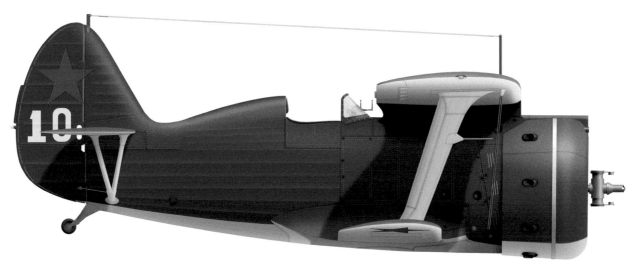

I-153 of the 160th IAP after overhaul at Factory No.1.

I-153 of the 160th IAP after overhaul at Factory No.1. The airplane was painted green overall on upper surfaces, insignia placed in four positions (wing undersides and vertical tail), according to the scheme attached to the SNK Directive No.1711.

Tail parts (two upper views) of MiG-3s manufactured by Factory No.1 in June – early July 1941. Insignia on fuselages and wing upper surfaces were painted over, the stars on the wing undersides were enlarged, the stars on the vertical tail were applied according to the scheme attached to the SNK Directive No.1711. For comparison, the lower view shows the tail part in a standard pre-war colour scheme and insignia on the fuselage.

MiG-3 fighters manufactured by Factory No.1 in June 1941. Insignia on fuselages and wing upper surfaces were painted over, the stars on the wing undersides were enlarged, stars on the vertical tail were applied according to the scheme attached to the SNK Directive No.1711.

3

VVS RKKA Aircraft Units
Application of Camouflages in Accordance With the Approved Scheme and Variety of Impromptu Paint Schemes

In accordance with the SNK Directive No.1711 'On camouflage painting of airplanes, runways, tents and airfield facilities' and, in particular, with its Appendix No.2 (NKO Order No.0043) (1), in late June 1941 the paint schemes and four instructions for covering aircraft with nondescript paints, designed for metal, wooden and fabric coverings, were sent to the VVS RKKA formations and units.

Instruction No.1
Painting with black camouflage paint 'AM-26' of metal upper surfaces of the airplanes, which have been painted in a 'protective' green colour.
1. *Insignia (stars) on the upper surfaces should be painted over. Insignia (stars) should be left on the tail fin only, according to the paint scheme attached hereto. The insignia on the lower surfaces remain unchanged.*
2. *All surfaces are to be prepared for painting in the following way:*
    (a) surfaces with grease stains must be washed with warm soapy water;
    b) the whole surface must be washed with clean water and wiped dry with clean flannel, chamois or soft rags.
3. *Painting must be performed indoors, if possible (outdoors also allowed), with minimal fluctuations in ambient conditions. The room temperature should be in the range of 18–23 °C and relative humidity up to 70%.*
4. *While painting outdoors, the same conditions of temperature and humidity should be observed if possible.*
5. *Avoid dust during the painting process.*
6. *The black masking paint 'AM-26' must be applied with a brush or a spray gun, according to the attached painting scheme.*
7. *Drying of the applied black paint 'AM-26' should be conducted at the temperature of 18–23 °C, for at least 24 hours.*
8. *Spray painting should be carried out, if possible, in a special room or compartments isolated from the premises by a tarpaulin partition to avoid the deposition of paint dust on other objects.*
9. *The air for spray painting must be filtered through an oil-and-water separator for removing dust, oil and moisture particles.*

Instruction No.2.
Painting with black camouflage nitro paint 'AMT-6' of the wooden and fabric wing upper surface, which have been painted in a 'protective' green colour.
1. *The insignia (stars) on the upper surfaces should be painted over. Insignia (stars) should be left only on the tail fin, according to the paint scheme attached hereto. The insignia on the undersides remain unchanged.*
2. *All surfaces are to be prepared for painting in the following way:*
    (a) airplanes with grease stains must be washed with warm soapy water;
    b) the whole surface must be washed with clean water and wiped dry with clean flannel, chamois or soft rags.
3. *Painting must be performed indoors, if possible (outdoors also allowed), with minimal fluctuations in ambient conditions. The room temperature should be in the range of 18–23 °C and relative humidity up to 70%.*
4. *While painting outdoors, the same conditions of temperature and humidity should be observed if possible.*
5. *Avoid dust during the painting process.*
6. *The black paint 'AM-26' must be applied in a single coat with a brush or a spray gun, according to the attached painting scheme.*
7. *Drying of the applied black paint 'AM-26' should be conducted at the temperature of 18–23 °C, for at least 2 hours.*

8. *Spray painting should be carried out, if possible, in a special room or compartments isolated from the premises by a tarpaulin partition to avoid the deposition of paint dust on other objects.*
9. *The air for spray painting must be filtered through an oil-and-water separator for removing dust, oil and moisture particles.*

Instruction No.3.
Painting with light green paint 'AM-24' of the metal wing upper surface, which have been painted in light (grey or aluminum) colour, followed by the application of black 'AM-26' camouflage paint.
1. *The insignia (stars) on the upper surfaces should be painted over. Insignia (stars) must be applied on the tail fin, according to the paint scheme attached hereto. The insignia on the undersides remain unchanged.*
2. *All surfaces are to be prepared for painting in the following way:*
    (a) *surfaces with grease stains must be washed with warm soapy water;*
    b) *the whole surface must be washed with clean water and wiped dry with clean flannel, chamois or soft rags.*
3. *The light green paint 'AM-24' and black paint 'AM-26' must be applied in a single coat with a brush or spray gun over the existing light (aluminum or grey) coating, according to the attached paint scheme.*
4. *The paints must be dried at 18–23°C for at least 24 hours.*
5. *Painting should be performed indoors, if possible (outdoors is also allowed), or in compartments isolated from the premises with a tarpaulin partition, to avoid fluctuations of ambient conditions. The room temperature should be within the range of 18–23°C at relative humidity up to 70%.*
6. *While painting outdoors, the same conditions of temperature and humidity should be observed if possible.*
7. *Avoid dust during the painting process.*
8. *The air for spray painting must be filtered through an oil-and-water separator for removing dust, oil and moisture particles.*

Instruction No.4
Painting with light green nitro-paint 'AMT-4' of the wing upper surface with wooden and fabric skin painted in white (aluminum) colour, followed by the application of camouflage black nitro-paint 'AMT-6'.
1. *The insignia (stars) on the upper surfaces must be painted over. Insignia (stars) must be applied on the tail fin, according to the paint scheme attached hereto. The insignia on the undersides remain unchanged.*
2. *All surfaces are to be prepared for painting in the following way:*
    (a) *surfaces with grease stains must be washed with warm soapy water;*
    b) *the whole surface must be washed with clean water and wiped dry with clean flannel, chamois or soft rags.*
3. *The light green paint 'AMT-4' and black paint 'AMT-6' must be applied in a single coat with a brush or spray gun over the existing light (aluminum or grey) coating, according to the attached paint scheme.*
4. *The paints must be dried at 18–23°C for at least 24 hours.*
5. *Painting should be performed indoors, if possible (outdoors is also allowed), or in compartments isolated from the premises with a tarpaulin partition, to avoid fluctuations of ambient conditions. The room temperature should be within 18–23°c at relative humidity up to 70%.*
6. *While painting outdoors, the same conditions of temperature and humidity should be observed if possible.*
7. *Avoid dust during the painting process.*
8. *The air for spray painting must be filtered through an oil-and-water separator for removing dust, oil and moisture particles.*

Moreover, a separate table provided for the approximate rates of paint consumption for different airplanes.

Thus, according to the calculations, camouflaging a single-engine airplane with metal skin which had been painted in 'protective' green colour required approximately 0.8 kg of black paint AM-26, and painting metal airplanes which had light colour (grey or aluminum) required 1.5 kg of green paint AM-24 and 0.8 kg of black paint AM-26. When painting single-engine airplane with wooden and fabric skin which had been covered with 'protective' green colour, about 9.0 kg of black paint AMT-6 was needed, and when painting airplanes covered in light colours – 9.6 kg of green paint AMT-4 and 9.0 kg of black AMT-6.

For twin-engine airplanes the requirements were as follows: for aircraft with metal surfaces painted in 'protective' green colour – 1.4 kg of black AM-26, and for metal airplanes painted in light colours – 3.8 kg of green AM-24 and 1.4 kg of black AM-26 paints. When painting twin-engine airplanes with wooden and fabric skin covered in 'protective' green paint it was necessary to use 21.0 kg of black AMT-6, and when painting airplanes covered in light colours – 22.4 kg of green AMT-4 and 21.0 kg of black AMT-6.

Of course, four-engine airplanes were also involved. All of them were all-metal. The aircraft which had been covered in 'protective' green colour required 3.5 kg of black paint AM-26, and the airplanes which had been covered in light colours needed 8.7 kg of green AM-24 and 3.5 kg of black AM-26 paints. (2)

These documents were received by the VVS RKKA units in early July, while the first known command on this subject – the order of the headquarters of the Southern Front Air Force, was signed on 3 July 1941. Indirect data shows that in other military districts and fronts similar orders were given on the same day. For instance, the photos attached to the accident reports of the 171st IAP clearly show that on 1 July the regimental aircraft were still painted in the pre-war scheme, while the airplane that crashed at 16:30 on 4 July 1941 had already been repainted by half. The deadlines for painting the camouflages and applying the insignia into the new positions were very tight. The tasks were to be completed by 10 July, so the personnel were forced to paint the airplanes literally in between combat or training sorties.

It is an interesting fact that in some Air Force units and formations the local orders to paint camouflages had probably been given even before the schemes and instructions were received. For example, the regiments of the 2nd SAD of the Northern Front Air Force began to camouflage the airplanes as early as 26 June (4). Naturally, such an approach made it unfeasible to ensure compliance with the schemes and instructions when painting. Usually, each regiment or formation applied the camouflages according to their own tastes and preferences. In addition, the photos show that painting the airplanes was done in haste, so it is often impossible to determine the colour as the spots were obviously not painted in black, and most of the regiments and divisions made no records on this matter.

Application of insignia was as liberal – often the stars on the vertical tail were not painted, and the insignia remained in the pre-war style of six positions.

In the regiments stationed at rear airfields and in training units the paint was applied more carefully – for example, the DB-3 manufactured in 1939, used by the Lipetsk aviation courses of improving the skills of squadron commanders. However, apparently due to the lack of a scheme, the insignia were also left in the 'old' positions.

On occasions, the camouflage pattern depended not even on the availability of paint, but on the artistic taste of a specific performer. In some cases, the improvised painting patterns strike with their amazing irregularities, as for example the camouflages of Il-2 ground attack aircraft, presumably of the 430th ShAP, abandoned because of malfunction at Shatalovo airfield in July 1941, of SB of an unknown unit abandoned on the enemy territory, or of UT-1 of the 286th IAP, crashed at Andreevka (Izyum) airfield on 18 August 1941. The exterior of these airplanes eloquently testifies to the considerable artistic ability of the persons who applied the camouflage.

It should be noted that at first little attention was paid to such 'insignificant things' as positioning and size of insignia. As a rule, regiments that had airplanes painted according to the standard of May 1940, at best, quickly applied black spots, and 'extra' fuselage stars were simply painted over. Around the first half of July, this was how the personnel of the 4th IAP painted their Il-2s. The photos of the regiment's airplanes with hastily applied black spots over the basic green on upper surfaces have recently been identified.

Many other airplanes at various sections of the front, from Leningrad to Odessa, were painted in a similar manner.

No less artfully were sometimes painted the airplanes in the regiments located in the rear districts. Most likely, in many units the 'ugly' plain black and green spots were replaced by good old 'Khalkhin-Gol' camouflages, which could consist either of combined black-and-green or of only single-colour green or black stains. Camouflage was applied both with a spray gun and by hand. Probably the lack of large stocks of black and green paints in bomber regiments, where there were still many silver and light-grey coloured airplanes, led to a surge of various improvisations in a style of a 'Khalkhin-Gol' camouflage and its variations. A typical example of the application of spots of different colours can be seen in the photo from the accident report of the SB from the 32nd-A SBAP (was later re-designated the 452nd SBAP).

Most often the silver or grey base colour was covered with small spots applied with a brush. This saved both time and paint.

The most practical servicemen simplified the task, painting over the insignia on the fuselage and upper surfaces with available green paint. It was typical not only of the Air Force units at the front line, but also in the rear, apparently due to the lack of necessary quantities of black paint. Thus, the personnel at the Air Force units from Belorussia to Kamchatka independently got to the same straightforward conclusions.

However, judging by the photos, a significant number of airplanes in the Air Force units operating at the front, which have liberally-applied camouflage, still received insignia in accordance with the scheme attached to the SNK Directive No.1711.

Probably the most predatory camouflage was painted on the MiG-3 fighters of the unknown regiment of the Northern Front Air Force, which were painted with thin black stripes over the basic green colour.

The units in rear districts also tried to follow the instructions for painting and applying the new insignia. Thus, while the DB-3/3f and TB-3 long-range and heavy bombers required a huge amount of paint, they were often painted in 'Khalkhin-Gol' camouflage, and the insignia were applied in accordance with the SNK Directive No.1711.

The personnel of many regiments and squadrons did not apply camouflage to the aircraft which had been painted in accordance with the instructions of May 1940. The insignia on the fuselages and wing upper surfaces were painted over, and the stars were applied on the vertical tails according to the scheme attached to the SNK Directive No.1711.

Painting large number of airplanes in unofficial improvised camouflage schemes with various positions of insignia was caused by objective factors. First, the units that had been instructed to switch to black-and-green camouflage had not received the instructions and schemes for about ten days. Second, the shortage of paints also had its negative impact. As a result, most of the Soviet airplanes captured by the Germans at the airfields and lost in the air battles and to anti-aircraft artillery fire in June–July 1941 were the non-camouflaged aircraft painted in the pre-war colours, with old insignia applied in six positions. But there are also many enemy photos of airplanes with improvised camouflages, retaining the insignia in six positions, or even in four positions in accordance with the new scheme. It is necessary to understand that the transition process took time. Even in the same unit there could be aircraft both with the old colour scheme and with improvised camouflage, and with the insignia applied in accordance with the new directive. The photos of aircraft belonging to the 12th SAD, abandoned at the airfield in Vitebsk can serve as a good example of the real state of things. Due to the rapid advance of the enemy troops these airplanes could not be evacuated to the rear.

After the schemes attached to SNK Directive No.1711 appeared *en masse* in the Air Force units, they were naturally used to paint the airplanes. Of course, due to the lack of templates with dimensions, the spots were often painted differently from the sample on the scheme and, as a result, there were practically no two aircraft with identical camouflage patterns. At the moment it is not possible to establish what paint types were used for camouflage, because there is no information about it in the documents of the regiments and divisions of the VVS RKKA.

Nevertheless, if not exactly by the date indicated in the documents, but within reasonable timeframes, many regiments managed to fulfil the task and put black-and-green camouflage and insignia in four positions on their aircraft according to the scheme attached to the SNK Directive No.1711.

A relatively small number of photos of aircraft painted in black-and-green camouflage and with the stars in four positions according to the scheme attached to the SNK Directive No.1711 can be attributed to objective factors. First – the short, about a week, period of such applicating the insignia. Already on 10 July 1941, units of the VVS RKKA received instructions to put stars of increased size in six positions. Secondly, it was due to the intensive combat operations taking place at that moment at the front and, as a consequence, the heavy losses incurred by the VVS RKKA. Nevertheless, it is clear that the process was initiated, and quite a lot of aircraft received the black-and-green camouflage in the recommended version.

For a long time, up until about 1944, the VVS RKKA units that were not part of the active army continued to paint the airplanes according to the scheme attached to the SNK Directive No.1711. However, airplanes were not always repainted in black-and-green camouflage. There were different variants, ranging from a simple painting over of the stars to the most original camouflage schemes at the Pacific Fleet Air Force. At that, the insignia were almost always applied in four positions. In addition, a number of factories located beyond the Urals and in the Central Asia, in particular Factories Nos.126, 84, and 23, continued to paint the insignia in accordance with the scheme attached to the SNK Directive No.1711.

One of the 'enclaves' in which the airplanes painted in black-and-green camouflage were kept in quite large numbers was the Central Asian Military District Air Force. Moreover, two trends were opposing each other inside the leadership of the district's Air Force. At the end of the summer of 1941 the units were divided into two roughly equal halves. At that, all the district's bomber regiments Nos. 1, 34, 458 and 459, as well as the 106th ShAP adopted and very thoroughly complied with the paint schemes attached to the SNK Directive No.1711. However, the fighter regiments as well as the 494th ShAP adhered to the self-styled silver camouflage, persistently applying it to the green-painted I-16s type 29 and I-153s of the late series. Actually, the airplanes of the 1st, 34th and 459th BAP were apparently the last aircraft painted in black-and-green camouflage with stars in four positions, which were transferred to the European part of the USSR and went into the action at the end of November 1941.

Summarizing this chapter, it should be noted that the issue of painting aircraft in VVS RKKA units, in accordance with the SNK Directive No.1711, remains resolved only partially. There is a huge gap in the types of the paints used, and it will probably no longer be possible to find an answer to this mystery.

List of documents employed:
1. ГАРФ, ф.5446, оп.106, д.20, л.31.
2. ЦАМО, ф.371, оп.6394, д.6, л.1–8.
3. ЦАМО, ф.2, САД, оп.1, д.7, л.8.
4. ЦАМО, ф.35, оп.11294, д.56, л.241–281.
5. ЦАМО, ф.35, оп.11294, д.62, л.151–171.
6. ЦАМО, ф.35, оп.11294, д.205, л.47–61.
7. ЦАМО, ф.35, оп.11294, д.62, л.57–67.
8. ЦАМО, ф.35, оп.11294, д.197, л.134–153.
9. ЦАМО, ф.35, оп.11294, д.202, л.314–340.
10. ЦАМО, ф.35, оп.11294, д.53, л.119–134.
11. ЦАМО, ф.35, оп.11294, д.183, л.507–520.
12. ЦАМО, ф.35, оп.11294, д.57, л.248–269.
13. ЦАМО, ф.35, оп.11294, д.190, л.333–347.
14. ЦАМО, ф.35, оп.11294, д.200, л.230–257.
15. ЦАМО, ф.35, оп.11294, д.200, л.270.

Schemes and colours of camouflage painting for single-engine and twin-engine airplanes, introduced by the SNK Directive No.1711 of 20 June 1941 as camouflage painting of the VVS RKKA aircraft.

I-153 s/n 6598 from the 171st IAP of the 77th SAD, Moscow Military District Air Force. On 1 July 1941, the airplane flown by Junior Lieutenant V.S. Artemyev crashed at Tula airfield.

I-153 s/n 6760 from the 171st IAP of the 77th SAD, Moscow Military District Air Force. On 4 July 1941, the airplane flown by Junior Lieutenant O.I. Shuvalov crashed at Tula airfield. The pilot died in the crash. (3)

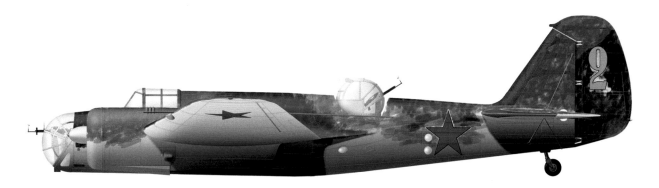

SB presumably from the 4th Squadron of the 44th SBAP.

SB, tactical number 2, presumably from the 4th Squadron of the 44th SBAP, abandoned at Grivochki airfield. The airplane was painted in improvised black-and-green camouflage with insignia applied in six positions according to the pre-war standard.

SB of the 2nd SBAP.

SB, tactical number 1, of the 2nd SBAP after a forced landing in the territory occupied by the enemy. The airplane was painted in improvised black-and-green camouflage with insignia applied in six positions according to the pre-war standard.

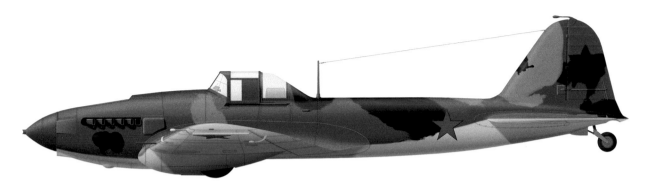

Il-2 presumably of the 232nd ShAP.

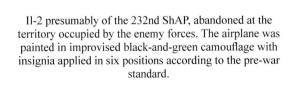

Il-2 presumably of the 232nd ShAP, abandoned at the
territory occupied by the enemy forces. The airplane was
painted in improvised black-and-green camouflage with
insignia applied in six positions according to the pre-war
standard.

I-16 type 5 s/n 521894 from the 154th IAP of the 39th IAD.

I-16 type 5 s/n 521894, tactical number 894, from the 154th IAP of the 39th Fighter Aviation Division (IAD, *Istrebitelnaya Aviatsionnaya Diviziya*) after a forced landing. The fighter was painted in improvised black-and-green camouflage with insignia applied in six positions according to the pre-war standard.

I-16, tactical number 2, of an unknown unit, captured at the place of forced landing, summer 1941. The aircraft was painted in improvised black-and-green camouflage with marks applied in six positions according to the pre-war standard.

Su-2, tactical number 16, of an unknown unit, captured at the place of forced landing, summer 1941. The airplane was painted in improvised black-and-green camouflage with insignia applied in six positions according to the pre-war standard.

DB-3 from the 1st Squadron of Lipetsk aviation courses of improving the skills of squadron commanders.

DB-3 s/n 391418, tactical number 7, from the Lipetsk aviation courses of improving the skills of squadron commanders. On 14 July 1941, the bomber flown by the Commander of the 1st Squadron, Major N.V. Ledenyov made an emergency landing at Lebedyan airfield. The airplane was painted in improvised black-and-green camouflage with insignia applied in six positions according to the pre-war standard. (5)

TB-3, tactical number 6, presumably of the
1st Heavy BAP, captured by the enemy at the
airfield. The bomber was painted in black-and-
green camouflage with the insignia applied in six
positions according to the pre-war standard.

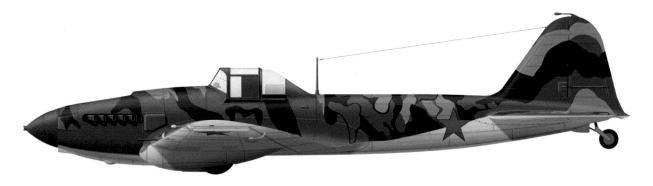

Il-2 presumably of the 430th ShAP.

Il-2 presumably of the 430th ShAP, painted in improvised black-and-green camouflage with insignia applied in six positions according to the pre-war standard.

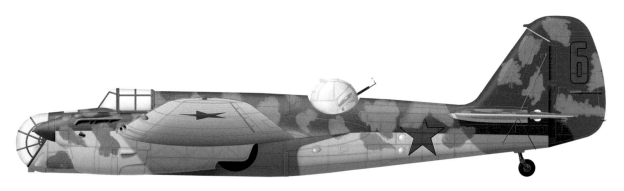

SB bomber presumably in Estonia, summer 1941.

SB, tactical number 6, captured by the enemy at the place of forced landing, summer 1941, presumably in Estonia. The airplane was painted in improvised camouflage with spots of light (most likely sandy) colour. Insignia applied in six positions according to the pre-war standard.

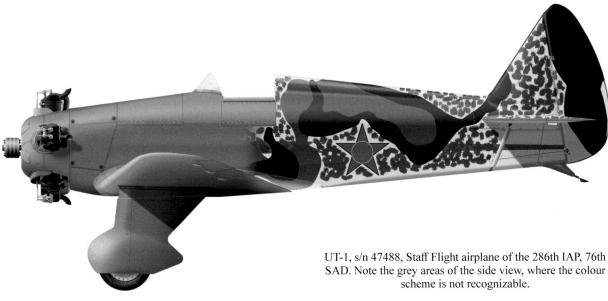

UT-1, s/n 47488, Staff Flight airplane of the 286th IAP, 76th SAD. Note the grey areas of the side view, where the colour scheme is not recognizable.

UT-1, s/n 47488, Staff Flight airplane from the 286th IAP of the 76th SAD. The aircraft flown by Deputy Regimental Commander, Battalion Commissar A.A. Largin was lost in a crash. The pilot died in the accident. The airplane was painted in black-and-green improvised camouflage, the gaps between the black-and-green spots were filled in with small spots. The insignia applied in six positions according to the pre-war standard. (6)

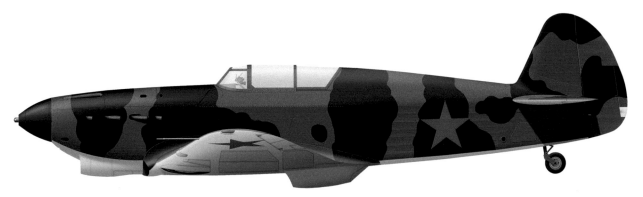

Yak-1 fighter of the 237th IAP, Orel airfield, 3 August 1941.

Yak-1 fighter s/n 1715 of the 237th IAP. On 3 August 1941, the fighter flown by Junior Lieutenant Mikhailov crashed at Orel airfield. The airplane was painted in improvised black-and-green camouflage with insignia applied in six positions according to the pre-war standard, the stars on the fuselage were carelessly painted over. (7)

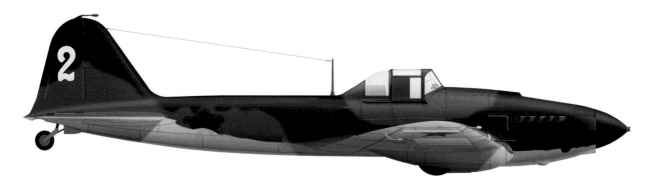

Il-2 from the 4th Squadron of the 4th ShAP, 11th SAD, July 1941.

Il-2 s/n 1862803, tactical number 2, from the 4th Squadron of the 4th ShAP, 11th SAD. The pilot, Squadron Commander Captain V.D. Lesnikov was missed in action on 20 July 1941. The airplane was painted in improvised black-and-green camouflage with insignia on the fuselage and wing upper surfaces painted over.

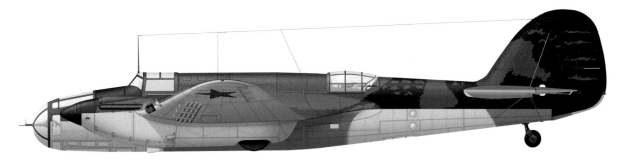

Ar-2 bomber of the 132nd SBAP, 45th SAD, Southern Front Air Force.

Ar-2 bomber from the 132nd SBAP of the 45th SAD, Southern Front Air Force, abandoned at Kirovograd airfield and captured by the enemy on 5 August 1941. The airplane was painted in black-and-green camouflage according to the scheme attached to the SNK Directive No.1711, the insignia on the fuselage and wing upper surfaces were painted over.

Pe-2 of the 2nd SBAP, 2nd SAD of the Northern Front Air Force, crashed in winter 1941. The airplane was painted in improvised black-and-green camouflage with insignia on the fuselage painted over.

Wreckage of SB s/n 39/8 (built by Factory No.125), tactical number 7, from the 1st Squadron of the 32nd-A SBAP, which crashed at Balashov airfield on 8 August 1941. The airplane was painted in so-called 'Khalkhin-Gol' camouflage over its basic silver colour. Note the different paints used – most likely green and black. (8)

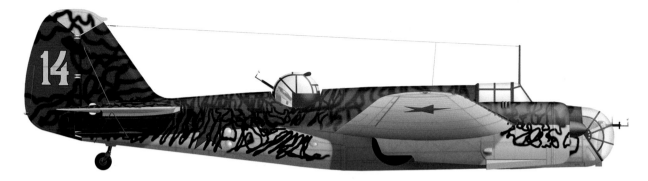

SB s/n 47/18 from the 2nd Squadron of the 454th SBAP, Undur-Khan airfield, 7 September 1941.

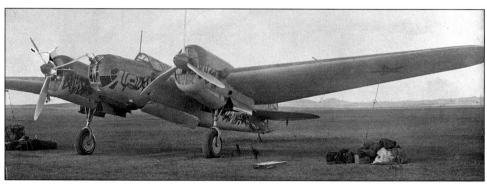

SB s/n 47/18 (built by Factory No.125), tactical number 14, from the 2nd Squadron of the 454th SBAP, flown by Lieutenant I.K. Tsvetkov. On 7 September 1941 the bomber was damaged in a collision with a wingman's airplane at Undur-Khan airfield. The airplane was painted in the so-called 'Khalkhin-Gol' camouflage scheme with black stripes over the basic green colour; the insignia on the fuselage were inaccurately painted over.

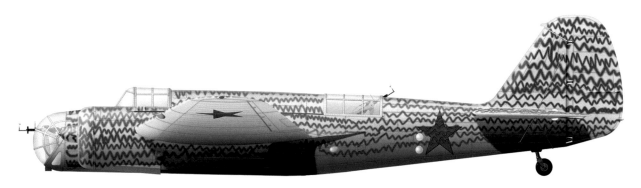

SB s/n 42/2 from the 2nd Squadron of the 454th SBAP, Undur-Khan airfield, 7 September 1941.

SB s/n 42/2 (built by Factory No.125) flown by Sergeant I.A. Bakanov from the 2nd Squadron of the 454th SBAP. The SB was damaged in a collision with wingman's airplane at Undur-Khan airfield on 7 September 1941. The airplane was painted in the so called 'Khalkhin-Gol' camouflage with green stripes over the basic silver colour, the insignia on the fuselage were inaccurately painted over. (9)

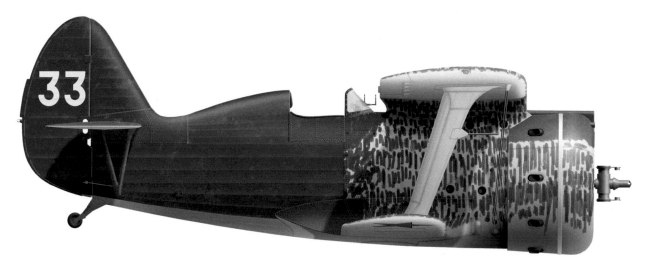

I-153 s/n 6465 from the 3rd Squadron of the 282nd IAP, 75th SAD, Kharkov Military District Air Force, Kremenchug airfield, 10 July 1941.

I-153 s/n 6465 from the 3rd Squadron, tactical number 33 of the 282nd IAP, 75th SAD, Kharkov Military District Air Force. On 10 July 1941, the airplane flown by Deputy Squadron Commander Lieutenant P.V. Bogatkov crashed at Kremenchug airfield. The fighter was probably painted in black-and-green improvised camouflage, the gaps between black and green areas were filled with smaller spots, with the fuselage insignia painted over. (10)

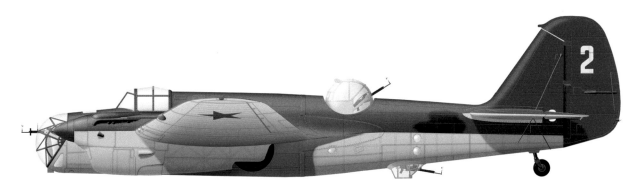

SB s/n 17/300 from the 2nd Squadron of the 71st Composite Aviation Regiment, Yelizovo airfield, 15 October 1941.

SB s/n 17/300, tactical number 2, from the 2nd Squadron of the 71st Composite Aviation Regiment, after an emergency landing at Yelizovo airfield (Kamchatka) on 15 October 1941. The airplane was painted with light green paint A-19f on the upper surfaces and blue A-18f on the undersides. Insignia on the fuselage and wing upper surfaces were painted over. (11)

DB-3f of an unknown unit, painted in improvised camouflage.

DB-3f, tactical number 10, of an unknown unit was shot down and landed at the enemy's territory. The airplane was painted in improvised camouflage of small black spots, insignia on the fuselage and wing upper surfaces were painted over, stars on the vertical tail were painted according to the scheme attached to the SNK Directive No.1711.

SB bombers, tactical numbers 1 and 6, of an unknown unit, were shot down in air combat or by enemy anti-aircraft fire. The airplanes were painted in the so-called 'Khalkhin-Gol' camouflage, the insignia on the fuselages and on the wing upper surfaces were painted over, the stars on the vertical tail were applied according to the scheme attached to the SNK Directive No.1711.

MiG-3s of the late series of an unknown unit of the Northern Front Air Force.

MiG-3s of the late series (from aircraft s/n 3501) of an unknown unit of the Northern Front Air Force were painted in improvised black-and-green camouflage, with insignia on fuselages and wing upper surfaces painted over; the stars were applied on the vertical tail in accordance with the scheme attached to the SNK Directive No.1711.

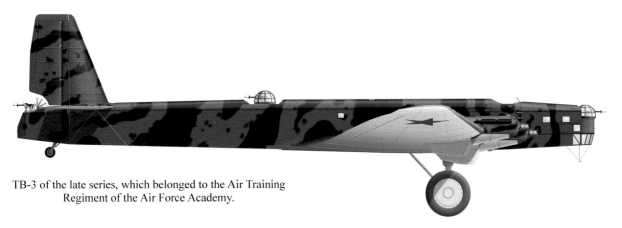

TB-3 of the late series, which belonged to the Air Training
Regiment of the Air Force Academy.

TB-3 of the late series, which belonged to the Air Training
Regiment of the Air Force Academy, was painted in improvised
black-and-green camouflage with insignia applied in accordance
with the scheme attached to the SNK Directive No.1711; the stars
on the fuselage and wing upper surfaces were painted over. (12)

The DB-3 s/n 180408 from the 2nd Squadron of the 445th SBAP, Bada airfield, 18 October 1941.

The DB-3 s/n 180408, tactical number 3, from the 2nd Squadron of the 445th SBAP. On 18 October 1941, the airplane flown by the Flight Commander Lieutenant I.K. Panchekhin crashed at Bada airfield. The airplane was painted in the so-called 'Khalkhin-Gol' camouflage, insignia on the fuselage and wing upper surfaces were painted over, the stars on the vertical tail were applied in accordance with the scheme attached to the SNK Directive No.1711. (13)

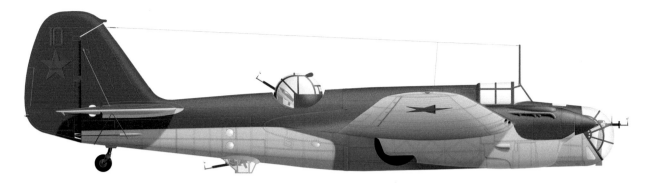

SB of the late series from the 128th SBAP, Vitebsk airfield.

SB of the late series, tactical number 10, from the 128th SBAP (transferred from the 6th SBAP after the beginning of the war). The aircraft made a forced landing at Vitebsk airfield. The upper surfaces were painted with light green paint A-19f, the undersides with blue A-18f. Insignia on the fuselage and wing upper surfaces were painted over and the stars on the vertical tail were applied according to the scheme attached to the SNK Directive No.1711.

SBs of the 6th and 128th SBAP, abandoned due to malfunctions at Vitebsk airfield. SB, tactical number 10, has pre-war camouflage and insignia in six positions. The airplane, tactical number 9, has pre-war camouflage and insignia in six positions, but with added small star added on the rudder. The airplane, tactical number 6, began to be painted either in 'Khalkhin-Gol' camouflage or simply in single-colour, similar to the SB without tactical number, but the process could not be completed. SB of the late series, tactical number 10 (small), has the insignia on the fuselage and wing upper surfaces painted over, but the star on the rudder was applied according to the scheme attached to the SNK Directive No.1711. The SB of the 96th series, without a tactical number, was originally painted in silver, and then repainted in green on upper surfaces, with stars in four positions according to the scheme attached to the SNK Directive No.1711.

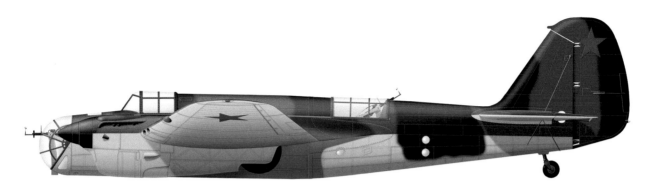

SB of an unknown unit painted according to the scheme attached to the SNK Directive No.1711.

SBs of an unknown unit painted in black-and-green camouflage with insignia applied in four positions according to the scheme attached to the SNK Directive No.1711.

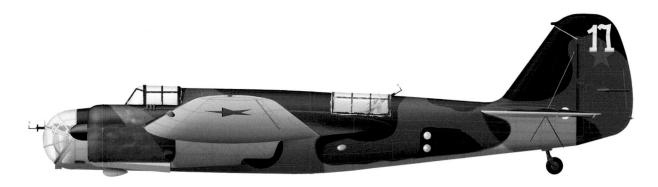

SB of an unknown unit painted according to the scheme attached to the SNK Directive No.1711.

SB, tactical number 17, of an unknown unit painted in black-and-green camouflage with insignia applied in four positions according to the scheme attached to the SNK Directive No.1711.

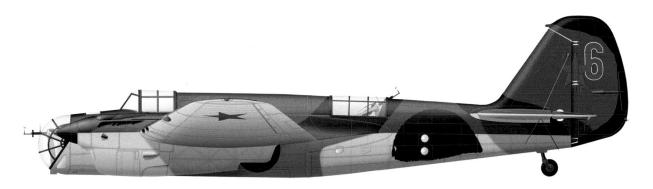

SB bomber from an unknown unit of the Southwestern Front Air Force, Ukraine, July 1941.

German servicemen are examining a downed SB bomber from an unknown unit of the Southwestern Front Air Force, Ukraine, July 1941. The airplane was painted in black-and-green camouflage with the insignia applied in four positions according to the scheme attached to the SNK Directive No.1711.

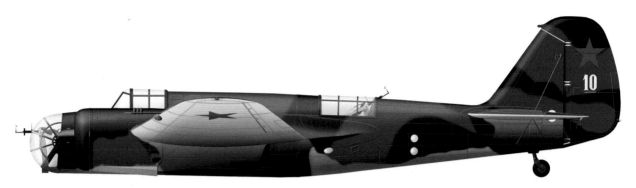

SB bomber from the 38th SBAP of the 10th SAD, Novgorod-Siverskiy airfield.

Centre and bottom: SB bomber, tactical number 10, from the 38th SBAP of the 10th SAD, abandoned due to damage at Novgorod-Siverskiy airfield. The airplanes were painted in black-and-green camouflage with insignia applied in four positions according to the scheme attached to the SNK Directive No.1711.

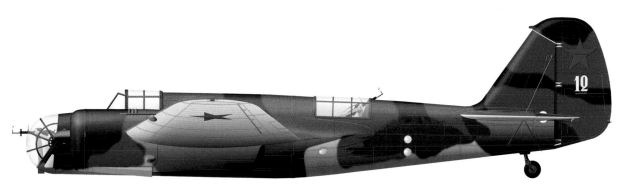

SB bomber from the 38th SBAP of the 10th SAD, Novgorod-Siverskiy airfield.

Centre and bottom: SB bomber, tactical number 12, from the 38th SBAP of the 10th SAD, abandoned due to damage at Novgorod-Siverskiy airfield. The airplanes were painted in black-and-green camouflage with insignia applied in four positions according to the scheme attached to the SNK Directive No.1711.

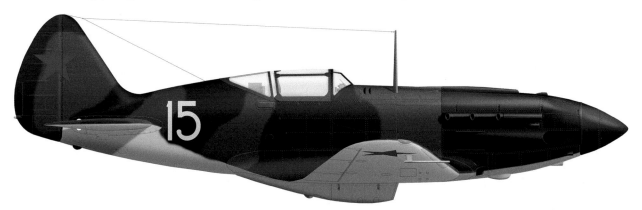

MiG-3 which was flown by Captain K.K. Kokkinaki, Commander of the 401st IAP, July 1941.

MiG-3 which was flown by Captain K.K. Kokkinaki, Commander of the 401st IAP in July 1941. The airplane was painted in black-and-green camouflage and had stars in four positions according to the scheme attached to the SNK Directive No.1711. Judging by the tactical number, originally this fighter was used by the 41st IAP.

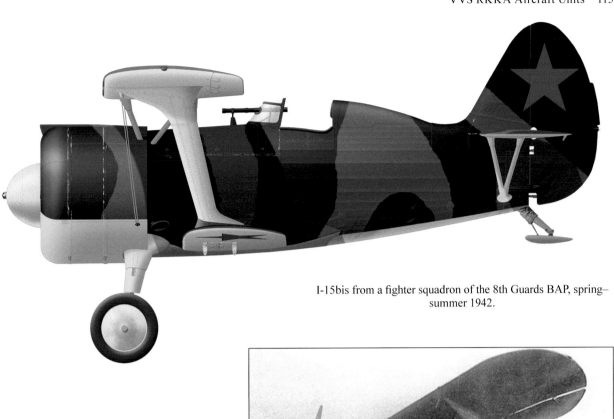

I-15bis from a fighter squadron of the 8th Guards BAP, spring–summer 1942.

I-15bis from a fighter squadron of the 8th Guards BAP, spring–summer 1942. The airplane was painted in black-and-green camouflage and had insignia in four positions according to the scheme attached to the SNK Directive No.1711.

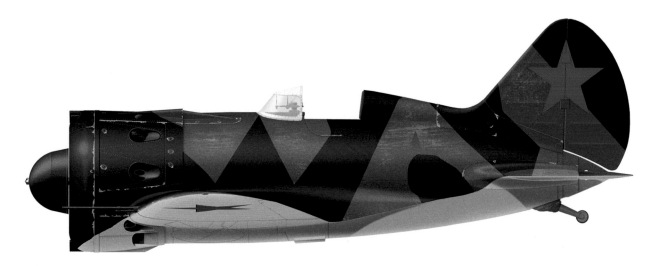

I-16 from the 178th IAP of 6th IAK of the Air Defense Forces.

I-16s from the 178th IAP of the 6th IAK of the Air Defense Forces. The airplanes were painted in black-and-green camouflage with insignia applied in four positions according to the scheme attached to the SNK Directive No.1711.

I-153 of an unknown unit, summer 1941.

I-153 of an unknown unit, summer 1941. The airplane was painted in black-and-green camouflage, with insignia applied in four positions according to the scheme attached to the SNK Directive No.1711.

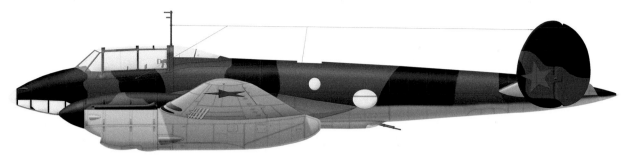

Pe-2 of the early series built by Factory No.22 from an unknown unit, summer 1941.

Pe-2s of the early series built by Factory No.22 from an unknown unit, summer 1941. The airplanes were painted in black-and-green camouflage, with insignia applied in four positions according to the scheme attached to the SNK Directive No.1711.

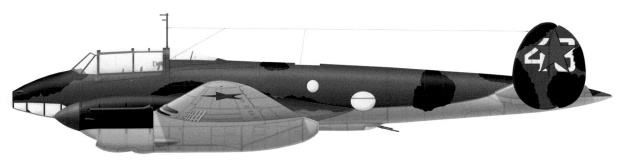

Pe-2 of the early series built by Factory No.39 of the 5th SBAP, August 1941.

Pe-2 of the early series built by Factory No.39, tactical number 48, of the 5th SBAP, which crash-landed near Babanka (Uman region) in August 1941. The airplane was painted in black-and-green camouflage with insignia applied in four positions according to the scheme attached to the SNK Directive No.1711.

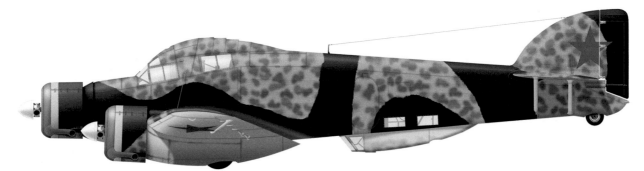

Ex-Yugoslavian SM-79 bomber from the Staff Flight of the 21st SAD.

Ex-Yugoslavian SM-79 bomber from the Staff Flight of the 21st SAD. The airplane was partially painted in black colour over the original camouflage, with insignia applied in four positions according to the scheme attached to the SNK Directive No.1711.

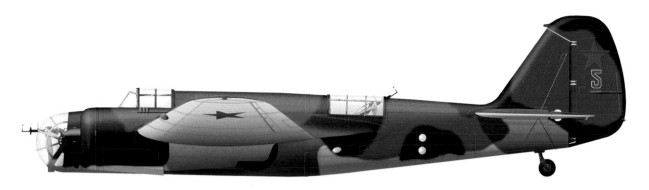

SB s/n 21/13 from the 2nd Squadron of the 458th BAP, 136th SAD. Ashkhabad airfield, 10 December 1941.

Collision of two airplanes from the 458th BAP of the 136th SAD, Ashkhabad airfield, 10 December 1941. The USB s/n 17/104, tactical number 2, flown by Deputy Commander of the 1st Squadron, Junior Lieutenant N.V. Puzanskiy, collided on landing with the SB s/n 21/13 (built by Factory No.125), tactical number 5, flown by the pilot of the 2nd Squadron, Junior Lieutenant A.Ya. Alyabyev. The airplanes were painted in black-and-green camouflage, with insignia applied in four positions according to the scheme attached to the SNK Directive No.1711. (14)

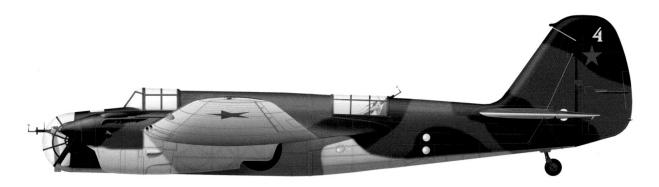

SB of the 34th SBAP, November 1941.

SB, tactical number 4, of the 34th SBAP was presumably lost during the flight to the Leningrad Front in November 1941.

Di-6 s/n 81242 from the 3rd Squadron of the 106th ShAP, 136th SAD, Ak-Tepe airfield, 12 November 1941.

Di-6 s/n 81242 built by Factory No.81, tactical number 8, from the 3rd Squadron of the 106th ShAP, 136th SAD. On 12 November 1941, the airplane flown by the pilot Sergeant A.Y. Chernyak made an emergency landing at Ak-Tepe airfield. (15)

4

Shaping the Final Look
Black-and-Green Camouflage and Enlarged Insignia in Six Positions

At the end of June/beginning of July 1941, in accordance with SNK Directive No.1711 (1), the NKAP factories switched to camouflage painting with nondescript paints and the application of insignia in four positions according to the instructions for painting attached to the Directive. On 18 July 1941 the NKAP approved the production instruction developed by VIAM – 'Main types of anti-corrosion protective coatings for land-based airplanes', which actually established dual-colour black-and-green camouflage of upper surfaces (oil paints AM-24 and AM-26 respectively for metal surfaces, and nitro paints AMT-4 and AMT-6 for wooden and fabric surfaces) and blue (AM-28 and AMT-7) for the undersides (2). Naturally, the process of transition to camouflage painting of aircraft at the factories and even more so in the VVS RKKA units was difficult and not instantaneous.

As it is described in detail in Chapters 2 and 3, due to the lack of time, the difficult situation at the fronts, and the shortage of new paints, it became impossible to achieve all the objectives of the SNK Directive No.1711 in the VVS RKKA units and formations as well as in some aircraft factories within the established timeframe. Somewhat later this process was complicated by quite unexpected circumstances. From the first days of the war, the VVS RKKA began to experience enormous problems due to the 'friendly fire'. Fighters and anti-aircraft gunners regularly fired at attacking airplanes, mistaking them for the enemy aircraft. This often resulted in losses of equipment and servicemen. The problem was very acute, and urgent measures were taken to solve it. In mid-July (the exact date is yet unknown), factories were instructed to apply insignia to the wing undersides and tailfins. For example, Factory No.22 began to apply enlarged stars starting from Pe-2 s/n 6/28 (3). However, this solution was apparently considered insufficient, and at a joint meeting of the Air Force Main Directorate and the NKAP, the decision was made to apply insignia of a larger diameter in addition to the insignia in four positions in order to facilitate identification of friendly aircraft:

Minutes of the conciliation meeting of 17 July 1941 (typed on 18 July 1941) on the placement of insignia (stars) on airplanes being delivered by the VVS RKKA Main Directorate.

Attendees:
- *from NKAP: Deputy People's Commissar of Aviation Industry Voronin;*
- *from VVS RKKA Main Directorate: Head of 10th Department, Brigade Engineer Bibikov.*

The following was agreed:
1. *In addition to the stars, applied according to the scheme approved by the Head of the VVS RKKA on the undersides of the wing and the side surfaces of the vertical tail, to apply stars on the sides of the fuselage.*
2. *The stars should be sized to fit into a circle of 1m in diameter.*
3. *All stars should be applied without black edging.*
4. *This decision is to be implemented immediately.* (4)

These documents were received by the aircraft factories the following day, on 19 July, and by the VVS RKKA units on 20 July. As an example, it is known that the order of the Headquarters of the 16th SAD of the Southwestern Front Air Force was signed in the morning of 20 July 1941, and received by the Headquarters of the 87th IAP at 12:25 on the same day – it required applying new insignia of enlarged size by 19:00 of the same day:

'According to instructions from the Head of the VVS RKKA Headquarters, the Commander of the 16th Air Division ordered:
1. *Stars must be applied on the airplanes: on the fuselage – 60cm, on the wings – 100cm on the undersides;*

2.   All works must be carried by the unit own forces and means.
3.   Completion must be reported by 19:00 on 20 July 1941.' (5)

The Aircraft Factory No.21 was the most disciplined among the NKAP factories, the same as in the case with implementation of previous assignments. The factory probably began to paint the aircraft according to the scheme approved by the SNK Directive No.1711 of 20 June 1941 and to apply the insignia without black edging in six positions at the beginning of the last decade of July. Unfortunately, the exact date and the airplane serial number, from which this application was started, were still not found in the records. Judging by the photos from accident and test reports, the aircraft starting from at least the 5th series (for example, airplanes s/ns 31215-55 and 31215-68), which were rolled out on 22–25 July 1941, have got the insignia on the fuselage. At that, the stars on the vertical tail apparently, remained small in size. Insignia of enlarged size on the vertical tail appeared on the airplanes no later than the 6th series. For example, they can be noted on the LaGG-3 s/n 31216-89 which underwent testing in August 1941.

Another important feature of painting the aircraft at the Factory No.21 was that the airplanes continued to be painted with alternating camouflage colours on every other airplane. The example of alternating colours can be clearly seen on the airplane s/n 31217-15, which underwent testing in August 1941.

It should be noted that the personnel of Factory No.21 continued to paint the aircraft according to the approved camouflage and to apply the insignia in six positions. The established scheme was used for two years and transferred from the LaGG-3 to the La-5, remaining unchanged until July 1943.

Taganrog-based Aircraft Factory No.31, which also produced LaGG-3 fighters, was the next enterprise that fulfilled the task almost by 100%. Painting of the airplanes with nitro paints started on 27 July 1941, so absolute majority of the airplanes (by then 11 LaGG-3 had been delivered to the Air Force and 25 to the Navy, and on 26 July six airplanes were in the process of acceptance) were painted in nitro paints AMT-4, AMT-6 and AMT-7, according to the scheme attached to the SNK Directive No.1711. The stars were applied in six positions, without black edging. The only deviation was application of a small star on the tail fin. Factory No.31 produced the LaGG-3 in this camouflage scheme for two years, and the smaller star on the vertical tail became a kind of hallmark of the airplanes built by the enterprise during the whole production. On the photos, this star allows to distinguish the aircraft built at Factory 31 from the aircraft manufactured by Factories Nos.21, 23, and 153.

Another enterprise that produced LaGG-3 fighters was Factory No.153. The aircraft were receiving black-and-green camouflage right at the factory, with insignia applied in six positions. However, the camouflage had deviations from the approved scheme. Most likely, the factory in Novosibirsk had no scheme available for a long time. Moreover, it is possible that the aircraft were painted with old paints, the leftovers from the time of UTI-4 production. An important feature of the airplanes produced at Factory No.153 was the application of insignia in the pattern similar to the one of Factory No.31, but the stars from Siberia were larger in size. The same approach was used for painting of later aircraft, such as the airplane of the 4th series s/n 0415321, which underwent testing in autumn 1941.

LaGG-3 fighters of Factory No.23 in Leningrad, judging by known photos (see Chapter 3), apparently did not get the insignia of the new system due to cease of production.

Originally, the Moscow-based Factory No.22 used new paints for camouflage application, but painting was done at the Central airfield. The applied spots generally complied with the approved scheme but were applied carelessly and lacked consistency from aircraft to aircraft. Nevertheless, the factory complied with the orders, and in late July the airplanes began to receive insignia in six positions, but with black edging. The quality of the camouflage did not radically change.

Judging by the photos, the new scheme began to be implemented starting from aircraft of the 30th–32nd series. The first clearly identifiable photos where enlarged stars can be seen were taken during tests of the rocket projectiles on Pe-2 s/n 16/32. The new insignia are clearly visible on the photos of testing Pe-2 s/n 10/35 and a heavy fighter version of the Pe-2 s/n 5/33. All these airplanes were built in early August 1941. Interestingly, all Pe-2s of the Factory No.22 carried similar camouflage and stars until the middle of 1943.

In late July, Factory No.39 continued its experiments by painting wavy camouflage on the Pe-2, which is described in detail in Chapter 2. The photos of captured Pe-2 s/n 391317 taken by German soldiers clearly show both camouflage and enlarged stars without black edging in six positions. Most likely, almost right up to the production of the last series of Pe-2s, the factory kept applying improvised camouflage schemes on its aircraft. Even the airplane s/n 391606 converted into a prototype of Pe-3 heavy fighter was apparently painted in wavy camouflage. It is yet unclear whether the camouflage was applied to the Pe-2 produced by Factory No.39 according to the scheme attached to the SNK Directive No.1711. Nevertheless, such possibility exists. For example, there exists an accident report of Pe-2 s/n 391702 of the 138th SBAP which, judging by photos of the vertical tail painting, probably received the standard black-and-green camouflage and stars in six positions. Moreover, one of the issues of *Soyuzkinojournal* newsreel, dedicated to the heroes of the 260th BAP, shows the aircraft produced by Factory No.39 that appears to be painted in black-and-green camouflage, in accordance with the scheme approved by the SNK Directive No.1711.

Aircraft Factory No.124 painted the airplanes in accordance with the black-and-green camouflage scheme approved by the SNK Directive No.1711, and in late July also switched to the scheme with insignia in six positions. At the same time, the size of the stars was smaller than on the Pe-2s of the Factories Nos.22 and 39. The first airplanes to receive the camouflage belonged to the 3rd and 4th series.

Production of Il-2 ground attack aircraft in summer 1941 was launched only at Factory No.18. The documents, which would detail painting of series production Il-2 airplanes, have not been discovered so far. However, numerous photos show a tendency to deviate from the scheme attached to the SNK Directive No.1711, and the degradation of camouflage painting of aircraft in late July. In Chapter 2 it was mentioned that no information was available on whether the ground attack airplanes had been painted at the factory or in the 1st Reserve Aviation Brigade, and what paints were used. Nevertheless, the airplanes of the 61st and 74th ShAP delivered to the frontline in the first half of July carried very thoroughly painted black-and-green camouflage according to the scheme attached to the SNK Directive No.1711 and insignia applied in four positions.

Some of the airplanes in standard camouflage received insignia, sometimes even enlarged ones, on the fuselage. These airplanes were probably the last to be camouflaged according to the scheme attached to the SNK Directive No.1711. Moreover, there is a possibility that the stars on the fuselage were painted right at the Air Force units.

Some of the early series aircraft received new insignia directly in the regiments. This is obvious from the improvised camouflages in which the ground attack airplanes were painted.

Starting from approximately 15–20 July, almost simultaneously with the implementation of the new system of applying enlarged insignia in six positions, the airplanes began to be painted in accordance with a simplified scheme. The first known aircraft to receive this simplified camouflage was photographed for the accident report of the 190th ShAP, dated 22 July 1941. (13) It is unknown why such decision was made, but up until the beginning of September 1941 16 regiments of ground attack aircraft painted in accordance with this simplified scheme were delivered to the frontline. Initially the star on the vertical tail was of a small size, but pretty soon, at least starting from the middle of the 11th series, it was enlarged. The camouflage was painted with alternating colours, which is clearly visible in the photo. There is a possibility that for some short period of time, perhaps just for a few days, the airplanes were painted in some sort of intermediate camouflage scheme where the spots on the wings and fuselage complied with the scheme attached to the SNK Directive No.1711, but were different on the vertical tail. Several airplanes were painted in this manner. However, just a few available photos do not provide sufficient background to make confident statements. There is a possibility that individual decisions were made, for example, during repairs.

It should be noted that already at the end of the first decade of August 1941, another transformation of camouflage scheme took place. On 21 August Soviet newsreel cameramen making the report about the combat operations of the 61st ShAP of the 47th SAD filmed the airplanes received for the regiment's reinforcement. For example, serial number and camouflage of the Il-2 s/n 1863514 can be seen on the newsreel footage. This is an aircraft of the 14th series, painted in an improvised black-and-green camouflage, not similar to any of the previously used ones. Its characteristic feature was a horizontal black stripe, usually of irregular shape, applied on the vertical tail. Enlarged insignia, including the tail star, were applied in six positions. According to other photos, the aircraft with this simplified camouflage had existed before, starting from the beginning of the 13th series. For example, the Il-2 s/n 182213 of the 243rd ShAP, which was shot down by anti-aircraft fire on 8 September 1941. It is still unclear what triggered this change of the paint scheme, which was mainly related to camouflaging of the tail unit. It was probably caused by the fact mentioned in Chapter 2: the airplanes were camouflaged not at the factory but at the site of the 1st Reserve Aviation Brigade where all the regiments that used Il-2 airplanes were formed at that time.

It is assumed that the transition to this camouflage came from a stricter scheme. At least one airplane, tactical number 20, was painted this way, with identical positions of insignia. Probably, the dramatically increasing number of regiments being formed and the consequent increase in the number of aircraft being transferred made the personnel paint the aircraft in haste, using approximate instructions and schemes, which resulted in yet another degradation of the camouflage.

At the end of the second decade and beginning of the third decade of August, the airplanes produced by Factory No.18 underwent a serious transformation. The camouflage was simplified even more. The scheme as such remained unchanged, but the black spots were probably painted randomly from airplane to airplane, and the typical horizontal black stripe of irregular shape on the vertical tail was gradually transforming into a shapeless spot. The final look of the Il-2s produced at the end of August – beginning of September 1941 was defined by unique insignia, which received a white edging. In addition, the star on the fuselage was reduced in size similar to the one on the pre-war aircraft.

For the first time, the mass appearance of the Il-2s with such camouflage scheme and application of insignia can be seen in the photos of aircraft of the 174th ShAP. The photos were taken in autumn 1941. The regiment received mostly the aircraft of the 21st series. It should be noted that the photographer captured one aircraft with stars of larger size on the fuselage. Probably it was one of the last airplanes with such a scheme of insignia application.

As it was mentioned in Chapter 2, the scheme of black-and-green camouflage, approved by the SNK Directive No.1711, was in fact the brainchild of the Yakovlev Design Bureau. However, Factory No.292 during the entire summer of 1941 was rolling out the Yak-1s in improvised black-and-green camouflage with serious deviations from the approved scheme. Moreover, the colouring according to the temporary scheme was very conventional and the spots applied to different airplanes were very noticeably different. The order to apply the new insignia to the fighter airplanes had been completed by the end of July, but situation with the camouflage had not been resolved by then.

The problem was apparently solved only in September, and it required the NKAP to issue the Order No.960cc of September 2, 1941: *'Recently the quality of finishing has deteriorated at Factory No.292. The main external finishing work is done by hand with brushes. I hereby order: I. To start airbrush painting of Yak-1 from 15 September 1941.'* (16)

This order was executed and starting from the second half of September the Yak-1 airplanes were released from the factory in standard black-and-green camouflage with enlarged insignia in six positions. It is likely that the camouflage, which followed the scheme attached to the SNK Directive No.1711, was introduced starting from the airplanes of the 35th–36th series.

In November 1941 the 62nd Fighter Aviation Brigade of the Black Sea Fleet Air Force received 13 Yak-1 airplanes of the 41st–42nd series, three of which in the early spring of 1942 became 'stars' in photos and film footage at Khersones airfield in Sevastopol. The photos and film clearly show that although the scheme of painting of the airplanes was the same, the areas of spots on all airplanes are a little bit different. This indicates the absence of special painting masks. Moreover, it is noticeable that the airplanes were initially painted entirely in green, and the black spots were applied over the basic colour. One of the Yak fighters, with tactical number 8, is camouflaged with alternating colours.

The airplanes of several subsequent series were painted in a similar fashion up until early December when the factory switched to the winter camouflage. It should be noted that several airplanes, having already been equipped with skis at the end of November, were still covered with black-and-green camouflage. One of those fighters made an emergency landing near the village of Barsuki (35km north-west of Mozhaisk). (17)

As it has been mentioned in Chapter 2, the Su-2 airplanes manufactured at Factory No.135 also received black-and-green camouflage, but so far no information has been found as to since what time which schemes were applied and which paints were used. Judging by the photos from accident reports and from the photos taken by the enemy, the airplanes were painted with significant deviations from the standard scheme. The distinguishing feature of the Su-2 aircraft of Factory No.135 became a small star applied on the rudder in a specifically defined place. After receiving instructions to paint enlarged insignia in six positions, this task was carried out, but up to the end of production the small star on the rudder remained in the same size.

By the end of July 1941, Factory No.126 in the Far East remained the only enterprise that was building DB-3f long-range bombers. Judging by the colours of the aircraft left at Orel airfield, no camouflage was applied by the factory at Komsomolsk-on-Amur for a long time at all. Due to the lack of records, it is impossible to establish exactly when the factory switched to painting the aircraft in black-and-green camouflage. Most likely it happened in the fall 1941, and it was definitely an improvised camouflage that didn't comply with the scheme attached to the SNK Directive No.1711. Moreover, the stars on the fuselage were missing. Up to the introduction of three-colour camouflage in summer 1943, the DB-3f/Il-4 bombers of Factory No.126 were manufactured exactly with such 'improvised' camouflage and with insignia applied in four positions.

Perhaps the only aircraft factory which produced airplanes of new types and which failed to introduce the black-and-green camouflage was in all senses the well-deserved Aircraft Factory No.1. The MiG-3 fighters manufactured by the enterprise did not receive the approved camouflage up until the end of serial production and continued to leave the factory in monochrome green colour on upper surfaces. At the same time, insignia changed from the order to the order, and application of enlarged stars in six positions was no exception. As a result, the black-and-green camouflages were applied to the MiG-3s directly at the Air Force units.

By the mid-August 1941, the majority of aircraft factories had mastered the black-and-green camouflage with new paints. By the end of September 1941, the bulk of the combat aircraft produced at the NKAP factories had been painted according to the scheme attached to the SNK Directive No.1711 and received enlarged insignia in six positions. These were the LaGG-3 fighters built by Factories Nos.21 and 31, the Yak-1 airplanes of Factory No.292, and the Pe-2 bombers of Factories Nos.22 and 124. The LaGG-3s of Factory No.153, the Pe-3s of Factory No.39, the Il-2s of Factory No.18, and the DB-3f's of Factory No.126 were still receiving improvised camouflages.

The Factory No.21 was an indisputable leader in terms of executing the orders on aircraft camouflaging: not only the new matte AMT nitro paints were used, but also the camouflage and insignia were applied carefully, according to the scheme attached to the SNK Directive No.1711.

The situation in the Air Force units was quite different. The majority of the RKKA VVS pre-war aircraft were lost in June–July 1941. Therefore, the opportunities of camouflaging combat airplanes were rapidly shrinking. Some of the equipment, which had come with the Air Force units from the Soviet internal districts and the Far East, as a rule was thrown into battle right upon arrival, so the personnel simply did not have the physical ability to apply the insignia and colouring in accordance with the orders. The order of 20 July 1941 to apply the insignia of increased size (60 cm on the fuselage, 100 cm on the undersides) provides for another marker that allows identification the aircraft of the summer–autumn 1941. The orders to apply the camouflage and insignia were executed in many military units, although, of course, in an improvised manner. As it had happened in late June and early July, many commanders took the path of least resistance. For example, the airplanes were often left in their old camouflage, but large insignia applied on the wings and fuselages, or stars were drawn on the tailfins in addition to the pre-war six-position arrangement.

However, there are many photos available showing aircraft without camouflage at all, or with carelessly applied insignia. The same formation could operate both camouflaged and non-camouflaged airplanes, either with insignia of enlarged size in six positions or with pre-war size stars. Regiments arriving from interior districts usually did not have time to apply the insignia and camouflage in compliance with the orders. In the same manner as in late June – early July, many combat units kept aircraft in their old camouflages, but put large insignia on the fuselage and wings, or painted a star on the tail in addition to the pre-war six-position insignia. As a result, a motley conglomerate of aircraft with multiple variations of camouflage and markings could appear in a single unit. But losses and wear and tear were taking their toll. There were fewer and fewer of the old airplanes left...

In the non-combatant districts and the Far Eastern Front, the situation was mostly similar to that of the active fronts. Many units and formations strictly followed orders and brought their aircraft into line with them. Interestingly, the order to put the enlarged insignia in six positions was not passed on to the districts, the Far Eastern Front and the Pacific Fleet at all. Therefore, the airplanes there remained with the small stars applied in four positions.

Notable things happened in some combat units – the 'protective' green camouflage was replaced with aluminum paint. It is known that this was done to the aircraft of the 167th IAP and the 492nd ShAP of the 137th SAD of the Central Asian Military District Air Force. In spring 1941, the 167th IAP received a set of brand new I-16 type 29 fighters, painted according to the scheme: green upper surfaces, light blue undersides. Some similarly painted aircraft of the 106th ShAP, including the I-153 airplanes of the late series, were transferred to the 492nd ShAP formed in August 1941. In August–September 1941 the airplanes of these regiments had already been completely repainted in silver colour.

The external look of the VVS RKKA aircraft for the next two years of the war actually took shape on 18–20 July 1941. It happened after the aircraft factories, in addition to painting new airplanes in black-and-green camouflage (in accordance with the scheme attached to the SNK Directive No.1711), began to apply insignia of enlarged size in six positions. Of course, the process was not going smoothly at the beginning, but by the winter of 1941 most enterprises had coped with the task and transferred to the approved scheme (or its variations), using nitro-paints of AMT-4/6/7 series or the AM-24/26/28 oil enamels. By this time very few pre-war built aircraft had remained in the active units of the Air Force. Though some individual aircraft in improvised camouflages operated in the combat units for a long time, they did not make much difference to the overall picture. Sometimes the aircraft mixture was made more colourful by the units, which were transferred from interior districts, or from the Russian Far East, but there is no doubt that the vast majority of military aircraft had standard, factory-applied camouflages. Only in internal districts as well as in relatively quiet sections of the front with many pre-war built airplanes, there were still a few camouflage systems that differed from the approved standards.

List of documents employed:
1. ГАРФ, ф.5446, оп.106, д.20, л.31.
2. V. Vakhlamov, M. Orlov, 'Colours of Soviet Aviation'. *M-Hobby* magazine, Issues 8/1997–5/1999.
3. ЦАМО, ф.35, оп.11287, д.16, л.212–214.
4. ГАСО, ф.Р-1261, оп.3, д.72, л.55.
5. ЦАМО, ф.87 ИАП, оп.2412, д.1, л.16.
6. ЦАМО, ф.35, оп.11294, д.59, л.76–89.
7. ЦАМО, ф.35, оп.11294, д.59, л.242–251.
8. ЦАМО, ф.35, оп.11294, д.201, л.266–273.
9. ЦАМО, ф.35, оп.11294, д.202, л.367–379.
10. ЦАМО, ф.35, оп.11294, д.64, л.112–127.
11. ЦАМО, ф.20420, оп.1, д.101, л.28–39.
12. ЦАМО, ф.35, оп.11294, д.197, л.346–368.
13. ЦАМО, ф.35, оп.11294, д.61, л.269–278.
14. ЦАМО, ф.35, оп.11605, д.5119, л.33–39.
15. ЦАМО, ф.35, оп.11605, д.5119, л.18–22.
16. РГАЭ, ф.8044, оп.1, д.1, л.1.
17. ЦАМО, ф.35, оп.11605 д.5120 л.78–92.
18. ЦАМО, ф.12290, д.162, л.22–24об.
19. ЦАМО, ф.12290, д.162, л.25–37.
20. ЦАМО, ф.35, оп.11294, д.200, л.201–204.
21. ЦАМО, ф.35, оп.11294, д.58, л.175–196.
22. ЦАМО, ф.35, оп.11294, д.57, л.248–269.
23. ЦАМО, ф.35, оп.11294, д.200, л.76–90.
24. ЦАМО, ф.35, оп.11294, д.46, л.131–138.
25. ЦАМО, ф.35, оп.11294, д.182, л.249–261.
26. ЦАМО, ф.492 ШАП, оп.396581, д.1, л.87–96.

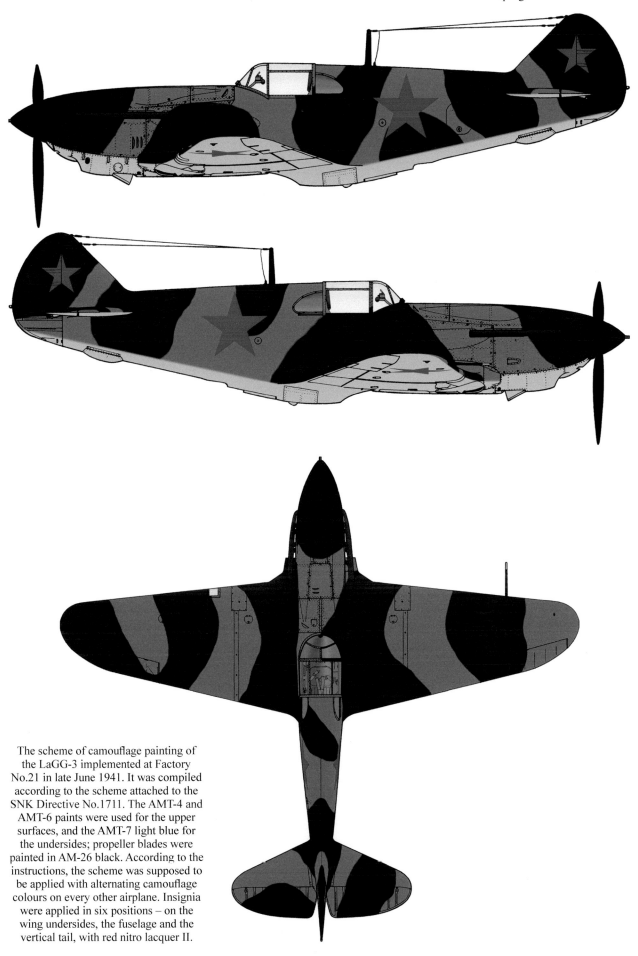

The scheme of camouflage painting of the LaGG-3 implemented at Factory No.21 in late June 1941. It was compiled according to the scheme attached to the SNK Directive No.1711. The AMT-4 and AMT-6 paints were used for the upper surfaces, and the AMT-7 light blue for the undersides; propeller blades were painted in AM-26 black. According to the instructions, the scheme was supposed to be applied with alternating camouflage colours on every other airplane. Insignia were applied in six positions – on the wing undersides, the fuselage and the vertical tail, with red nitro lacquer II.

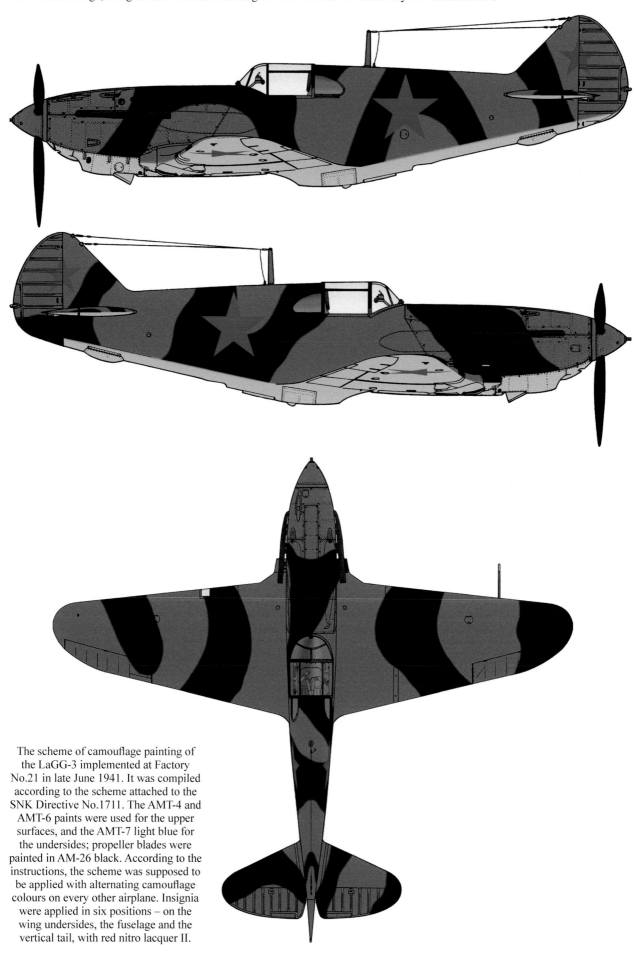

The scheme of camouflage painting of the LaGG-3 implemented at Factory No.21 in late June 1941. It was compiled according to the scheme attached to the SNK Directive No.1711. The AMT-4 and AMT-6 paints were used for the upper surfaces, and the AMT-7 light blue for the undersides; propeller blades were painted in AM-26 black. According to the instructions, the scheme was supposed to be applied with alternating camouflage colours on every other airplane. Insignia were applied in six positions – on the wing undersides, the fuselage and the vertical tail, with red nitro lacquer II.

LaGG-3, s/n 31214-22, painted in black-and-green camouflage, according to the scheme attached to the SNK Directive No.1711. The AMT-4 and AMT-6 paints were used for the upper surfaces, and the AMT-7 light blue for the undersides. Insignia applied in six positions – on the wing undersides, the fuselage and the vertical tail, with a small star on the vertical tail. The airplane was used to test rocket projectiles.

LaGG-3 painted in black-and-green camouflage, according to the scheme attached to the SNK Directive No.1711. The AMT-4 and AMT-6 paints were used for the upper surfaces, and the AMT-7 light blue for the undersides. Insignia applied in six positions – on the wing undersides, the fuselage and the vertical tail, with a small star on the vertical tail. The airplane crash landed.

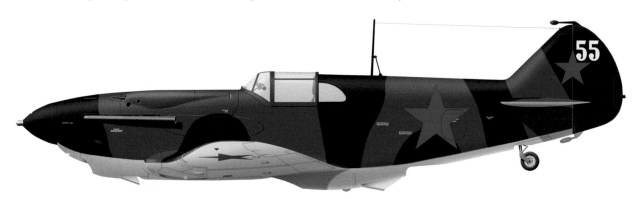

LaGG-3 s/n 31215-55 of the 2nd ZAP, Seyma airfield, August 1941.

LaGG-3 s/n 31215-55 of the 2nd ZAP was lost in a crash on 14 August 1941 at Seyma airfield when flown by a pilot of the 434th IAP Lieutenant A.S. Savich. The airplane was painted in black-and-green camouflage. The AMT-4 and AMT-6 paints were used for the upper surfaces, and the AMT-7 light blue for the undersides, with propeller blades painted in AM-26 black. Insignia applied in six positions – on the wing undersides, the fuselage and the vertical tail. (6)

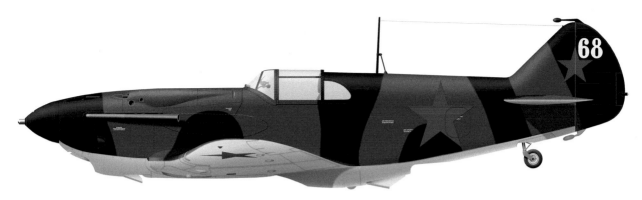

LaGG-3 s/n 31215-68 of the 2nd ZAP, Seyma airfield, 9 September 1941.

LaGG-3 s/n 31215-68. On 9 September 1941, the fighter flown by the Junior Lieutenant A.N. Shakuro from the 2nd ZAP crashed at Seyma airfield. The AMT-4 and AMT-6 paints were used for the upper surfaces, and the AMT-7 light blue for the undersides, with propeller blades painted in AM-26 black. Insignia applied in six positions – on the wing undersides, the fuselage and the vertical tail. (7)

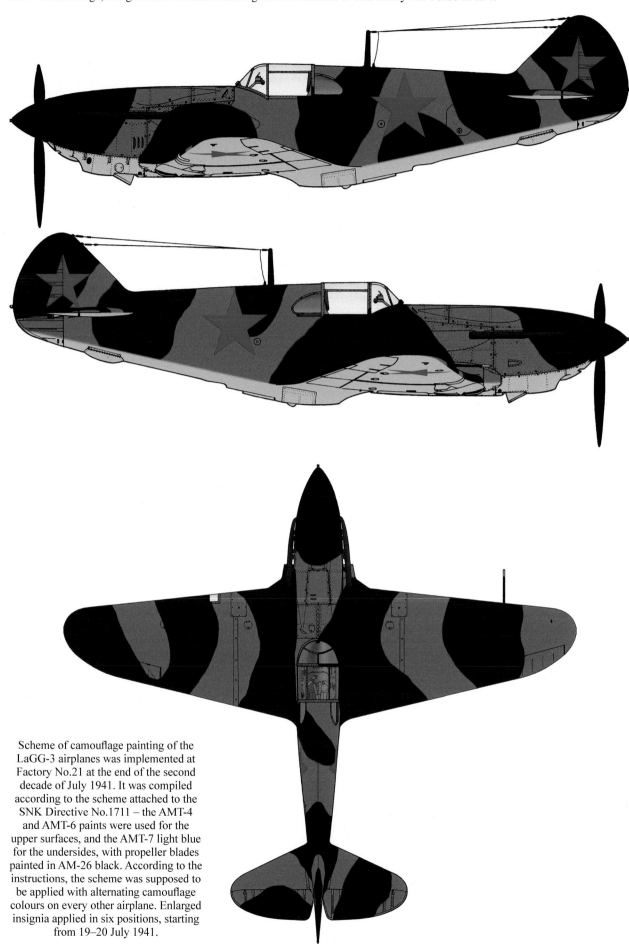

Scheme of camouflage painting of the LaGG-3 airplanes was implemented at Factory No.21 at the end of the second decade of July 1941. It was compiled according to the scheme attached to the SNK Directive No.1711 – the AMT-4 and AMT-6 paints were used for the upper surfaces, and the AMT-7 light blue for the undersides, with propeller blades painted in AM-26 black. According to the instructions, the scheme was supposed to be applied with alternating camouflage colours on every other airplane. Enlarged insignia applied in six positions, starting from 19–20 July 1941.

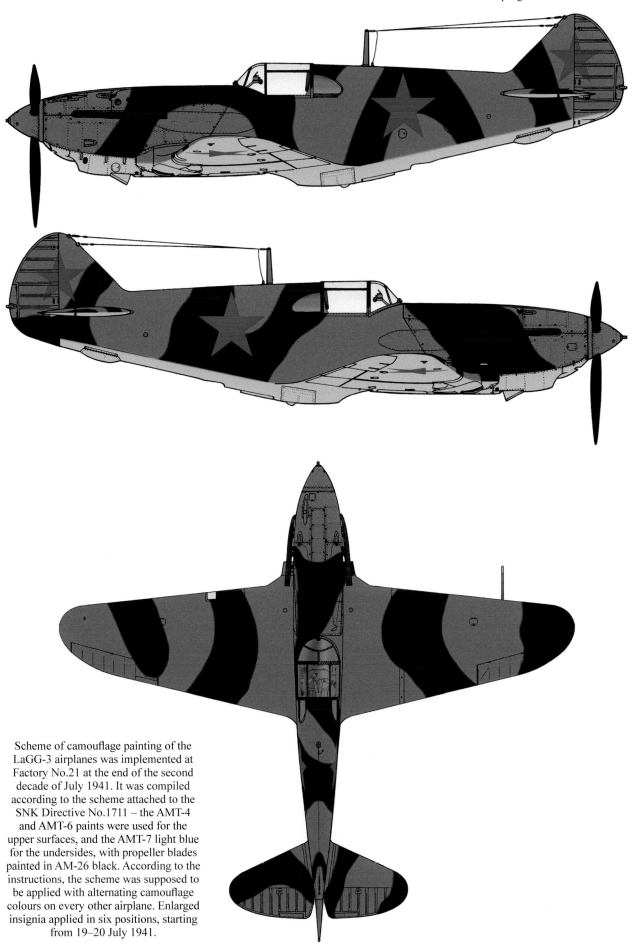

Scheme of camouflage painting of the LaGG-3 airplanes was implemented at Factory No.21 at the end of the second decade of July 1941. It was compiled according to the scheme attached to the SNK Directive No.1711 – the AMT-4 and AMT-6 paints were used for the upper surfaces, and the AMT-7 light blue for the undersides, with propeller blades painted in AM-26 black. According to the instructions, the scheme was supposed to be applied with alternating camouflage colours on every other airplane. Enlarged insignia applied in six positions, starting from 19–20 July 1941.

LaGG-3 built by Factory No.21, tactical number 460. The airplane was painted in black-and-green camouflage, according to the scheme attached to the SNK Directive No.1711. The AMT-4 and AMT-6 paints were used for the upper surfaces, and the AMT-7 light blue for the undersides. The insignia of the increased size were applied in six positions. The airplane was captured by the enemy at the place of forced landing. The fighter presumably belonged to the 46th IAP, 8th IAD, August–September 1941.

LaGG-3 s/n 31217-15 during testing, August 1941. The airplane was painted in black-and-green camouflage, with colour spots alternated as comparing to the prescribed camouflage scheme. Insignia were applied in six positions, with an enlarged star on the vertical tail.

LaGG-3, tactical number 71, of the 524th IAP, captured by Finnish soldiers at the place of forced landing in winter 1941–1942. The airplane was painted in black-and-green camouflage, with alternating colour spots. The insignia applied in six positions with an enlarged star on the vertical tail.

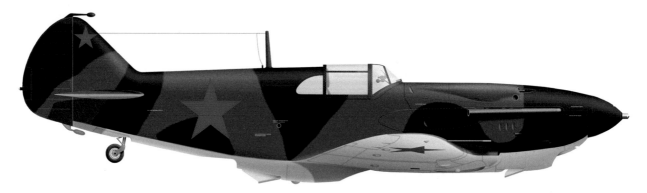

Scheme of camouflage painting of the LaGG-3 airplanes was implemented at Factory No.31 in late June 1941. It was compiled according to the scheme attached to the SNK Directive No.1711 – the AMT-4 and AMT-6 paints were used for the upper surfaces, and the AMT-7 light blue for the undersides; propeller blades were painted in AM-26 black. Insignia applied in six positions – on the wing undersides, the fuselage and the vertical tail with red nitro lacquer II.

LaGG-3 s/n 263124 of 11th ZAP, flown by Junior Lieutenant M.T. Laptinov, after crash at Rostov-on-Don airfield on 27 August 1941. The airplane of the first series was completed by the Factory No.31 on 27 July 1941. This is one of the first LaGG-3 painted in black-and-green standard camouflage. The AMT-4 and AMT-6 paints were used for the upper surfaces, and the AMT-7 light blue for the undersides, with propeller blades painted in AM-26 black. Insignia applied in six positions with red nitro lacquer II. (8)

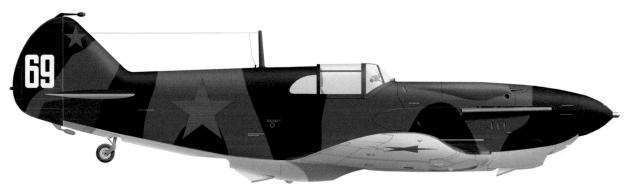

LaGG-3, tactical number 69, of an unknown unit.

LaGG-3, tactical number 69, manufactured by Factory No.31. The airplane was painted in black-and-green standard camouflage – the AMT-4 and AMT-6 paints were used for the upper surfaces, and the AMT-7 light blue for the undersides. This airplane of an unknown unit was captured by the enemy at the site of forced landing.

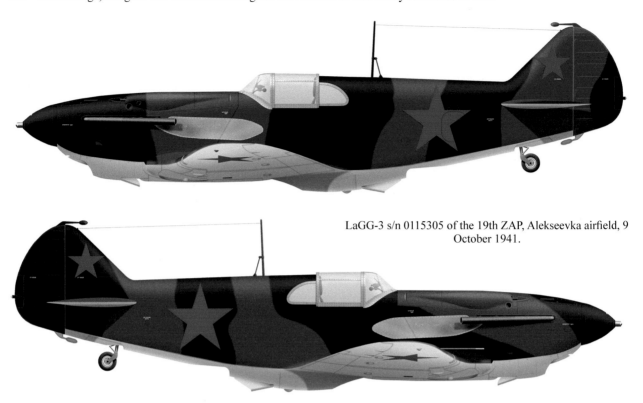

LaGG-3 s/n 0115305 of the 19th ZAP, Alekseevka airfield, 9 October 1941.

LaGG-3 s/n 0115305 of the 19th ZAP. On 9 October 1941 the fighter piloted by Junior Lieutenant I.M. Shcherba crash landed at Alekseevka airfield. The airplane of the first series built at Factory No.153, was rolled out on 23 August 1941, and painted in factory improvised black-and-green camouflage with stars applied in six positions. (9)

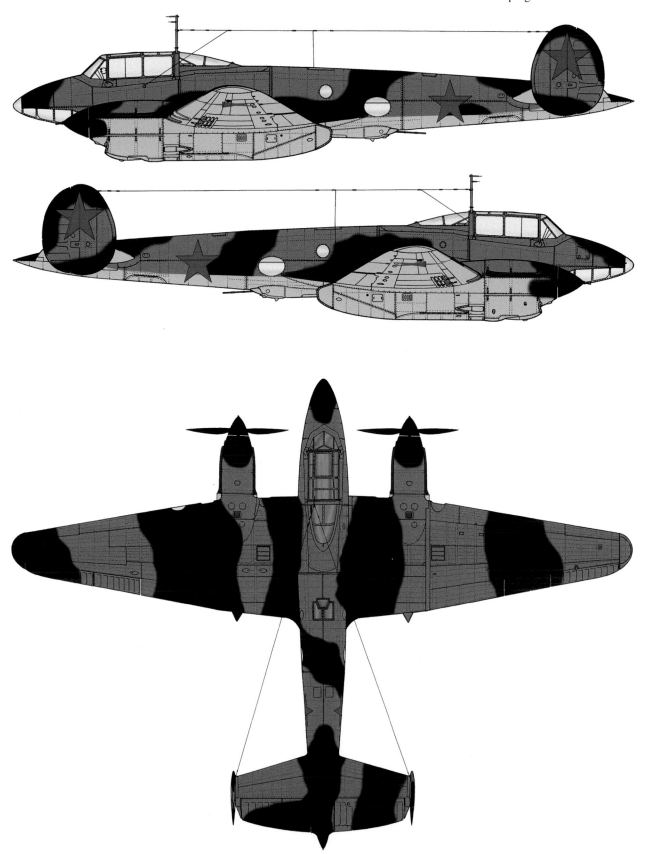

Scheme of camouflage painting of Pe-2 airplane implemented at Factory No.22 in late July 1941. It was compiled according to the scheme attached to the SNK Directive No.1711. The AM-24 and AM-26 paints were used for the upper surfaces, and the AM-28 light blue for the undersides. Insignia applied in six positions – on the wing undersides, the fuselage and the vertical tails.

Pe-2s s/ns 16/32, 5/33 and 10/35 during testing, August 1941. The airplanes were painted in black-and-green camouflage, according to the scheme attached to the SNK Directive No.1711. The AM-24 and AM-26 paints were used for the upper surfaces, and the AM-28 light blue for the undersides; propeller blades were painted in AM-26 black. Insignia of increased size with black edging were applied in six positions; red nitro lacquer II was employed.

Pe-2 s/n 20/40 from the 1st Squadron of the 507th SBAP crashed at Gryazi airfield on 15 September 1941. The pilot Sergeant Ya.S. Vlasov and the navigator Junior Lieutenant A.I. Tikhiy suffered no injuries, the gunner/radio operator Sergeant I.P. Lazarev was slightly wounded. The airplane was completed on 2 September 1941, painted in black-and-green camouflage, according to the scheme attached to SNK Directive No.1711. The AM-24 and AM-26 paints were used for the upper surfaces, and the AM-28 light blue for the undersides; propeller blades were painted in AM-26 black. Insignia with black edging were applied in six positions, using red nitro lacquer II. (10)

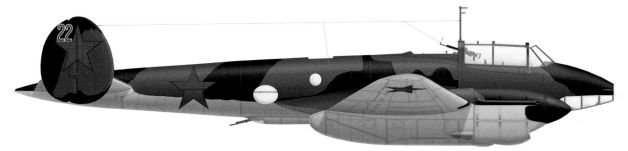

Pe-2 of an unknown unit, presumably in Ukraine, August–September 1941.

Above and top of page overleaf: Pe-2 of an unknown unit, captured by the enemy in August–September 1941, presumably in Ukraine. The airplane was produced in early August 1941, painted in black-and-green camouflage, according to the scheme attached to the SNK Directive No.1711. The AM-24 and AM-26 paints were used for the upper surfaces, and the AM-28 light blue for the undersides; propeller blades were painted in AM-26 black. Enlarged insignia with black edging were applied in six positions, using red nitro lacquer II. (11)

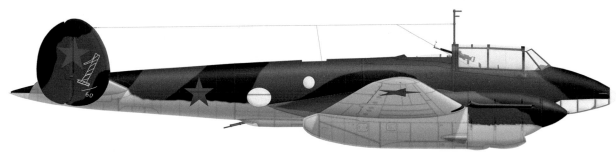

Pe-2 s/n 605 from the 3rd Squadron of the 15th ZAP, 30 September 1941.

Pe-2 s/n 605 (5th airplane of the 6th series), tactical number 1, built by Factory No.124, from the 3rd Squadron of the 15th ZAP. On 30 September 1941, the airplane flown by Lieutenant V.A. Shalnykh was damaged in a crash. The pilot was slightly wounded. The Pe-2 was painted in black-and-green camouflage, according to the scheme attached to the SNK Directive No.1711, with insignia applied in six positions. (12)

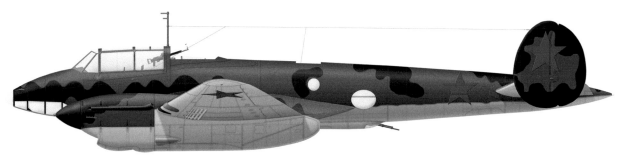

Pe-2 presumably of the 13th series
s/n 391317.

Pe-2 presumably of the 13th series s/n
391317, captured at the airfield. The
airplane was built by Factory No.39,
painted in improvised black-and-green
camouflage with enlarged insignia applied
in six positions.

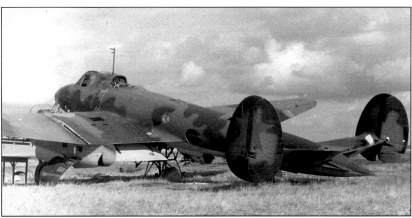

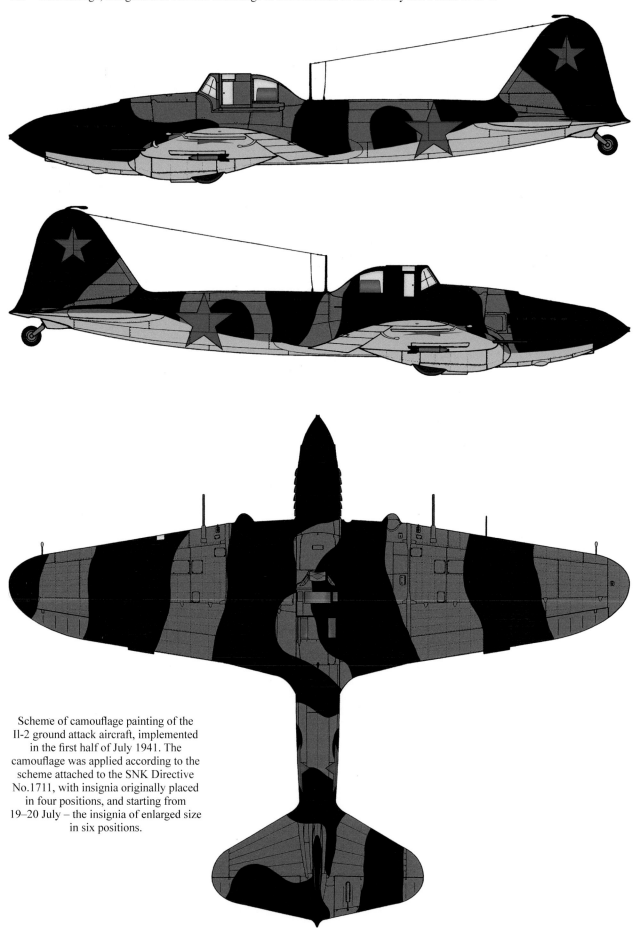

Scheme of camouflage painting of the Il-2 ground attack aircraft, implemented in the first half of July 1941. The camouflage was applied according to the scheme attached to the SNK Directive No.1711, with insignia originally placed in four positions, and starting from 19–20 July – the insignia of enlarged size in six positions.

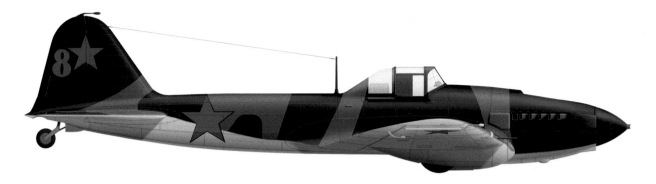

Il-2 of an unknown unit, July–August 1941.

Il-2, tactical number 8, of an unknown unit, captured by the enemy at an airfield, July–August 1941. The airplane was painted in standard black-and-green camouflage according to the scheme attached to the SNK Directive No.1711, with the insignia of the average size applied on a fuselage.

Il-2, tactical number 4, of an unknown unit, captured by the enemy at the place of forced landing, July–August 1941. The airplane was painted in standard black-and-green camouflage according to the scheme attached to the SNK Directive No.1711, with the insignia of the increased size applied on the fuselage.

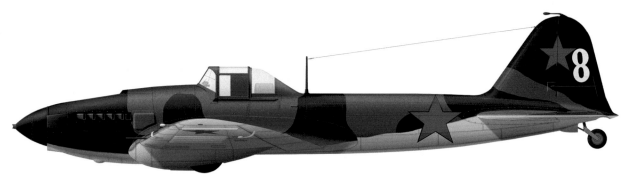

Il-2 s/n 1860211, July–August 1941.

Il-2 s/n 1860211, tactical number 8, captured by the enemy at the place of forced landing, July–August 1941. The airplane was painted in standard black-and-green camouflage according to the scheme attached to the SNK Directive No.1711, with enlarged insignia applied on the fuselage.

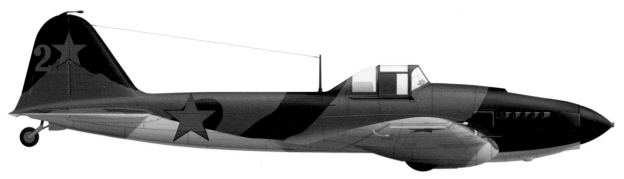

Il-2 s/n 1864208 of an unknown unit.

Il-2 s/n 1864208, tactical number 2, captured by the enemy
at the airfield. The airplane was painted in improvised
black-and-green camouflage with enlarged insignia on the
fuselage.

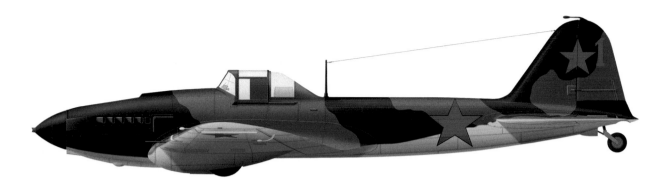

Il-2 of an unknown unit, 31 July 1941.

Il-2, tactical number 1, captured by the enemy at the place of forced landing near Shatalovo, 31 July 1941. The airplane was painted in improvised black-and-green camouflage with enlarged insignia on the fuselage.

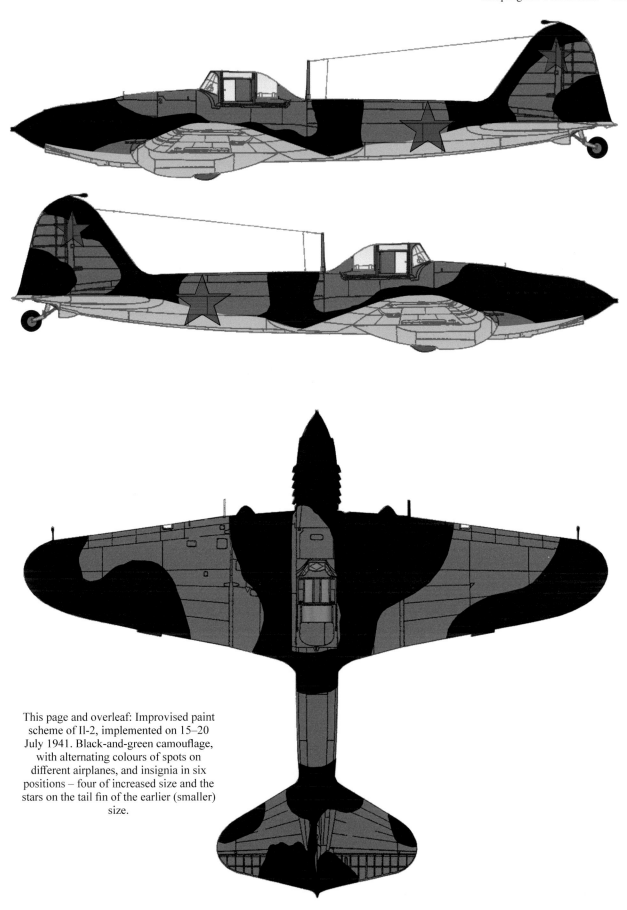

This page and overleaf: Improvised paint scheme of Il-2, implemented on 15–20 July 1941. Black-and-green camouflage, with alternating colours of spots on different airplanes, and insignia in six positions – four of increased size and the stars on the tail fin of the earlier (smaller) size.

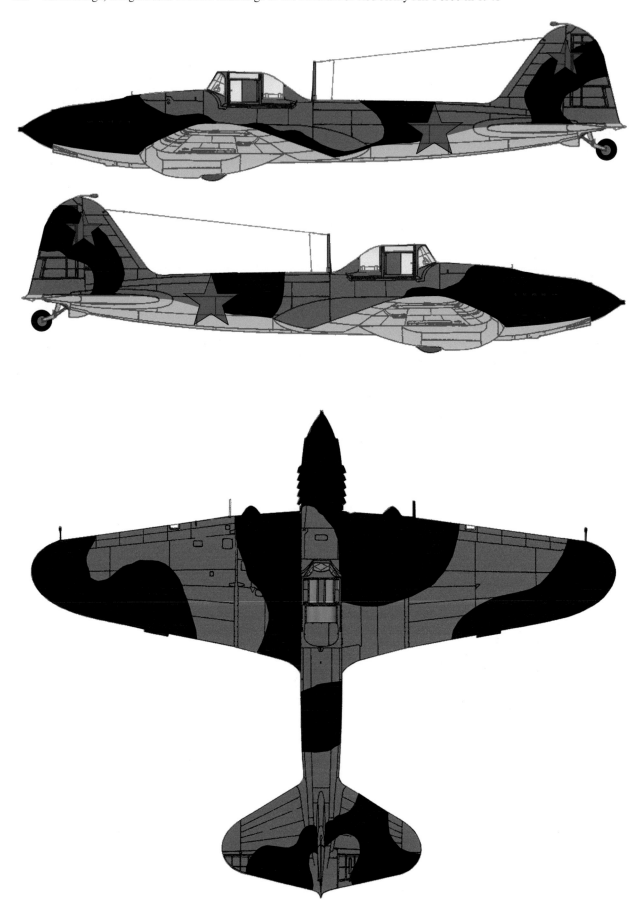

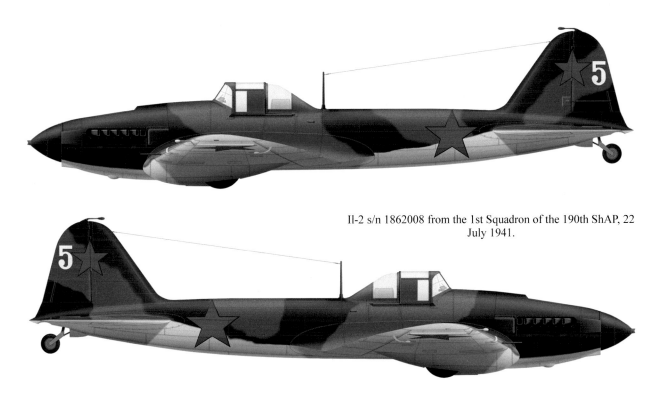

Il-2 s/n 1862008 from the 1st Squadron of the 190th ShAP, 22 July 1941.

Il-2 s/n 1862008, tactical number 5, from the 1st Squadron of the 190th ShAP, crashed during a ferry flight to the frontline at an airfield near Voronezh, 22 July 1941. The pilot, Lieutenant K.A. Skvortsov and Junior Military Technician A.I. Mogilev died. The airplane was painted in improvised black-and-green camouflage applied at Factory No.18, with insignia in six positions – four of increased size and the stars on the tail fin of the earlier (smaller) size.

Il-2 of an unknown unit, August–September 1941.

Il-2, tactical number 2, of an unknown unit, captured by the enemy at the place of forced landing, August–September 1941. The airplane was painted in improvised black-and-green camouflage, with insignia in six positions – four of increased size and the stars on the tail fin of the earlier (smaller) size.

Il-2, tactical number 8, of an unknown unit, captured by the enemy at the airfield, August–September 1941. The airplane was painted in improvised black-and-green camouflage, with insignia in six positions – four of increased size and the stars on the tail fin of the earlier (smaller) size.

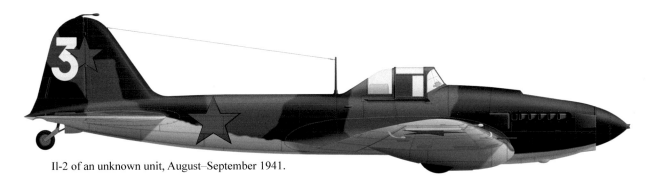

Il-2 of an unknown unit, August–September 1941.

Il-2, tactical number 3, of an unknown unit, captured by the enemy at the place of forced landing, August–September 1941. The airplane was painted in improvised black-and-green camouflage, with insignia in six positions – four of increased size and the stars on the tail fin of the earlier (smaller) size.

Il-2, tactical number 5, of an unknown unit, captured by the enemy at the place of forced landing, August–September 1941. The airplane was painted in improvised black-and-green camouflage, with insignia in six positions – four of increased size and the stars on the tail fin of the earlier (smaller) size.

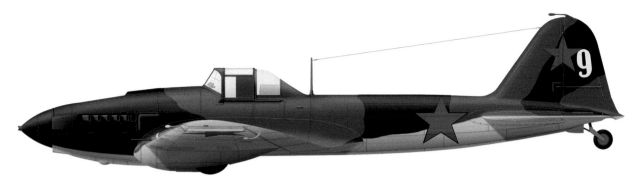

Il-2 of an unknown unit, July–August 1941.

Il-2, tactical number 9, of an unknown unit, captured by the enemy at the place of forced landing, July–August 1941. The airplane was painted in improvised black-and-green camouflage, with alternating colours and insignia in six positions – four of increased size and the stars on the tail fin of the earlier (smaller) size.

Il-2 of an unknown unit, captured by the enemy at the place of forced landing, August–September 1941. The airplane was painted in improvised black-and-green camouflage, with alternating colours and insignia in six positions – four of increased size and the stars on the tail fin of the earlier (smaller) size.

Il-2 of an unknown unit, captured by the enemy at the place of forced landing, August–September 1941. The airplane was painted in improvised black-and-green camouflage, with alternating colours and insignia in six positions – four of increased size and the stars on the tail fin of the earlier (smaller) size.

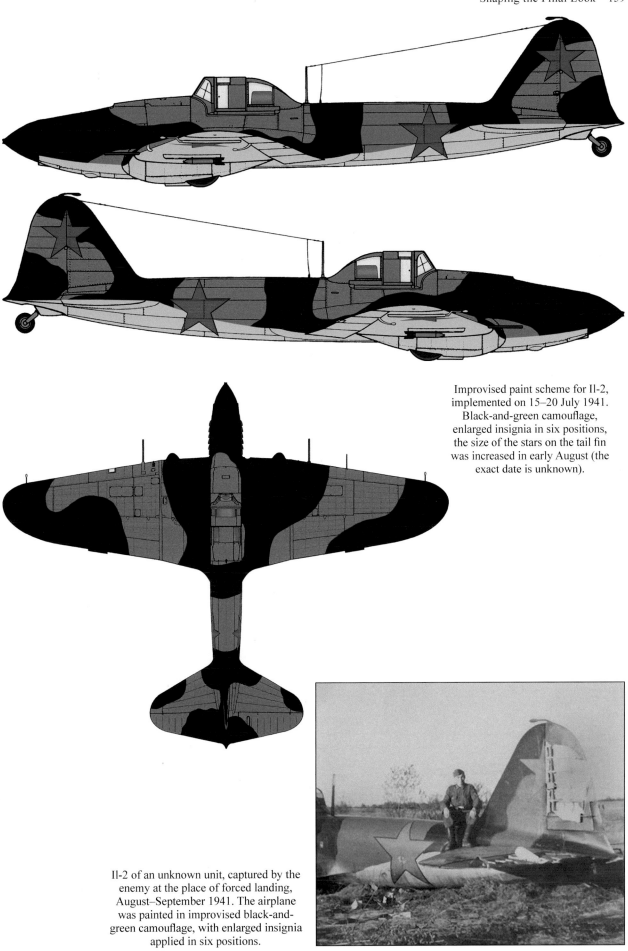

Improvised paint scheme for Il-2,
implemented on 15–20 July 1941.
Black-and-green camouflage,
enlarged insignia in six positions,
the size of the stars on the tail fin
was increased in early August (the
exact date is unknown).

Il-2 of an unknown unit, captured by the
enemy at the place of forced landing,
August–September 1941. The airplane
was painted in improvised black-and-
green camouflage, with enlarged insignia
applied in six positions.

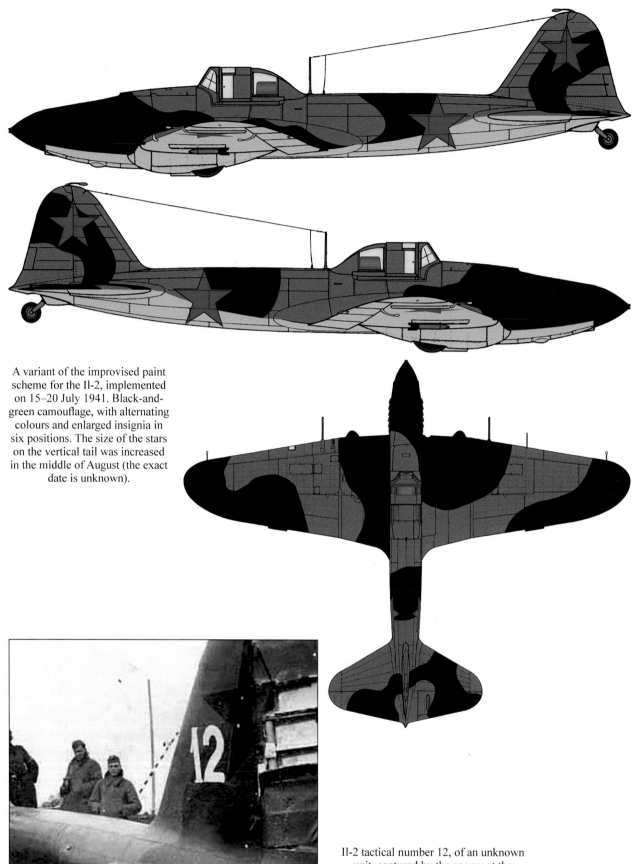

A variant of the improvised paint scheme for the Il-2, implemented on 15–20 July 1941. Black-and-green camouflage, with alternating colours and enlarged insignia in six positions. The size of the stars on the vertical tail was increased in the middle of August (the exact date is unknown).

Il-2 tactical number 12, of an unknown unit, captured by the enemy at the place of forced landing, July–August 1941. The airplane was painted in the improvised black-and-green camouflage, with alternating colours and enlarged insignia in six positions.

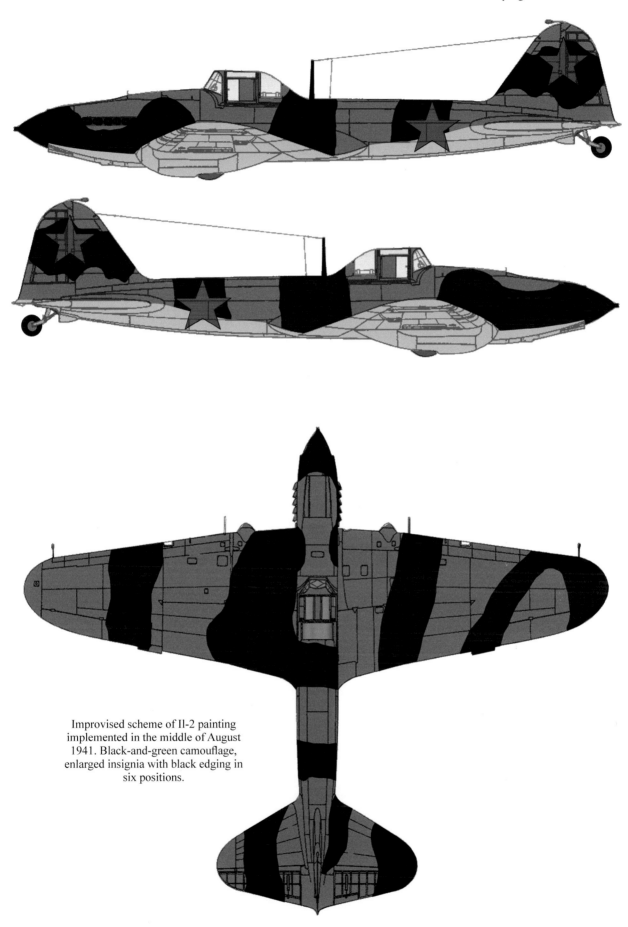

Improvised scheme of Il-2 painting
implemented in the middle of August
1941. Black-and-green camouflage,
enlarged insignia with black edging in
six positions.

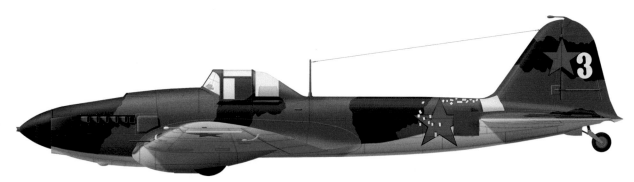

Il-2 s/n 1863514 of the 61st ShAP, August 1941.

Il-2 s/n 1863514, tactical number 3, from the 61st ShAP, August 1941. The airplane was painted in improvised black-and-green camouflage of the Factory No.18, with enlarged insignia applied in six positions.

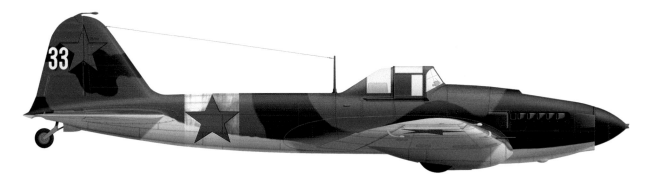

Il-2 s/n 2213 of the 243rd ShAP, September 1941.

Il-2 s/n 2213, tactical number 33, of the 243rd ShAP. On 8 September 1941, the aircraft flown by Junior Lieutenant I.G. Kiryukhin was shot down by anti-aircraft fire.

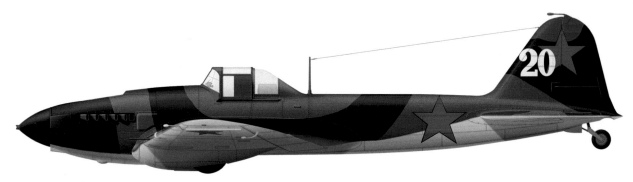

Il-2 of an unknown unit, autumn 1941.

Il-2, tactical number 20, of an unknown unit, captured by the enemy at an airfield, autumn 1941. The airplane was painted in improvised black-and-green camouflage of the Factory No.18, with enlarged insignia applied in six positions.

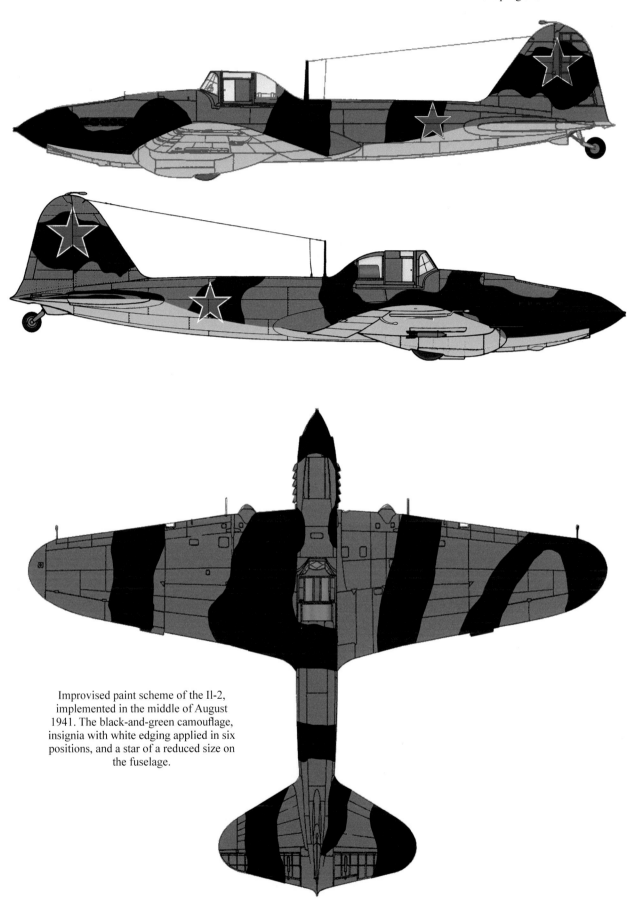

Improvised paint scheme of the Il-2, implemented in the middle of August 1941. The black-and-green camouflage, insignia with white edging applied in six positions, and a star of a reduced size on the fuselage.

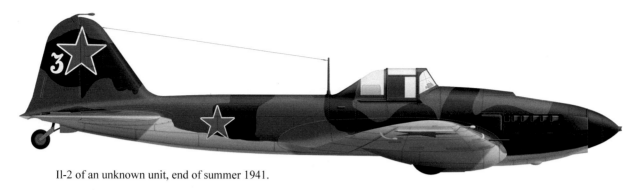

Il-2 of an unknown unit, end of summer 1941.

Il-2, tactical number 3, manufactured at the end of summer 1941, painted in improvised black-and-green camouflage. The vertical tail still had a horizontal black stripe of irregular shape, insignia with white edging applied in six positions, and a star of reduced size on the fuselage.

Il-2, tactical number 3, manufactured at the end of summer 1941, painted in improvised black-and-green camouflage. The vertical tail still had a horizontal black stripe of irregular shape, insignia with white edging applied in six positions, and a star of reduced size on the fuselage.

Il-2, tactical number 7, manufactured at the end of summer 1941, painted in improvised black-and-green camouflage. The vertical tail still had a horizontal black stripe of irregular shape, the insignia with white edging applied in six positions, and a star of reduced size on the fuselage.

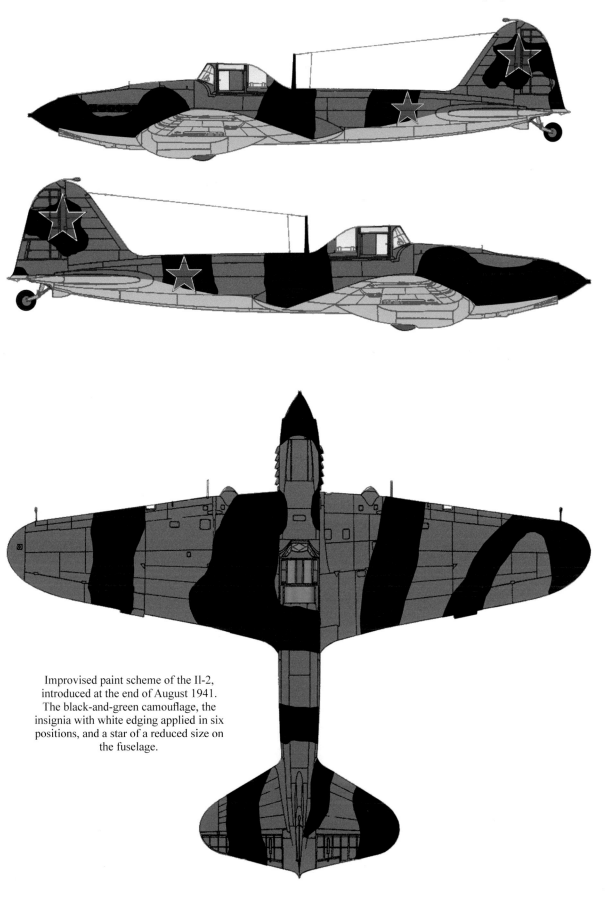

Improvised paint scheme of the Il-2,
introduced at the end of August 1941.
The black-and-green camouflage, the
insignia with white edging applied in six
positions, and a star of a reduced size on
the fuselage.

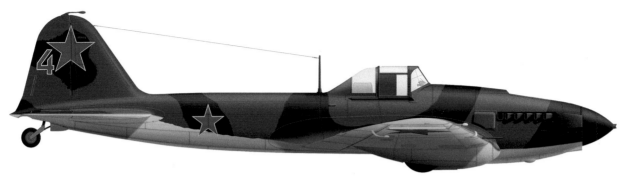

Il-2 s/n 1864818 of an unknown unit.

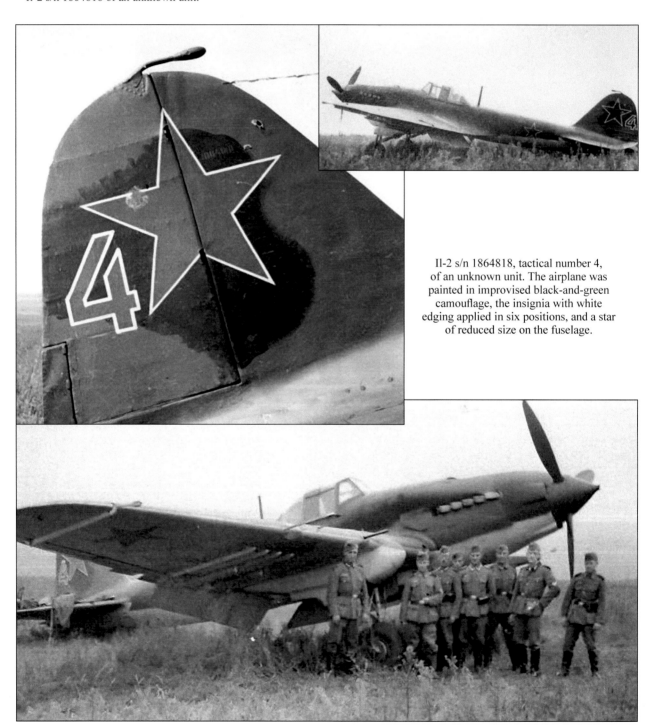

Il-2 s/n 1864818, tactical number 4, of an unknown unit. The airplane was painted in improvised black-and-green camouflage, the insignia with white edging applied in six positions, and a star of reduced size on the fuselage.

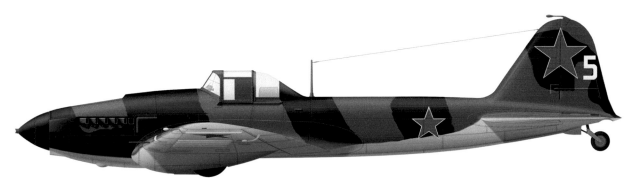

Il-2 of an unknown unit.

Il-2, tactical number 5, of an unknown unit. The airplane was painted in improvised black-and-green camouflage, the insignia with white edging applied in six positions, and a star of reduced size on the fuselage.

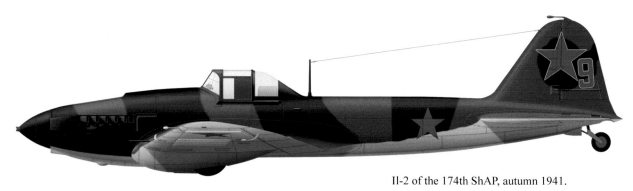

Il-2 of the 174th ShAP, autumn 1941.

Il-2, tactical number 9, of the 174th ShAP, autumn 1941. The airplane was painted in improvised black-and-green camouflage, the insignia with white edging applied in six positions, and a star of reduced size on the fuselage.

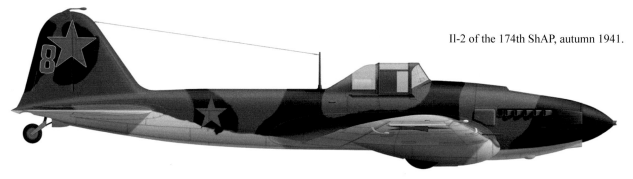

Il-2 of the 174th ShAP, autumn 1941.

Il-2, tactical number 8, of the 174th ShAP, autumn 1941. The airplane was painted in improvised black-and-green camouflage, the insignia with white edging applied in six positions, and a star of reduced size on the fuselage.

Yak-1 s/n 1823 of the 163rd IAP, July 1941.

Yak-1 s/n 1823, tactical number 104, of the 163rd IAP. On 27 July 1941, the airplane flown by the Commander of the 1st Squadron of the 163rd IAP, Captain I.S. Shulyak made a forced landing. The airplane was painted in the improvised black-and-green camouflage of Factory No.292, with enlarged insignia applied in six positions. (14)

Yak-1 s/n 1730 of the 237th IAP, August 1941.

Yak-1 s/n 1730, tactical number 32, of the 237th IAP. On 18 August 1941, the fighter flown by Deputy Commander for Political Affairs of the 237th IAP, Battalion Commissar N.S. Kiselev made a forced landing while flying from the Bagay-Baranovka airfield (Volsk) to the frontline. The airplane was painted in the improvised black-and-green camouflage of Factory No.292, with enlarged insignia applied in six positions. (15)

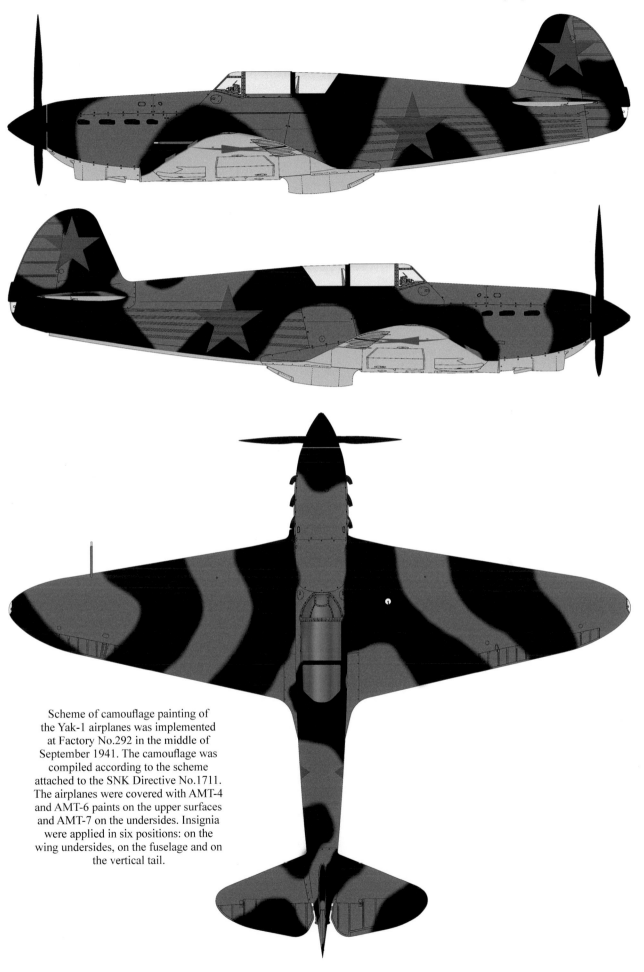

Scheme of camouflage painting of the Yak-1 airplanes was implemented at Factory No.292 in the middle of September 1941. The camouflage was compiled according to the scheme attached to the SNK Directive No.1711. The airplanes were covered with AMT-4 and AMT-6 paints on the upper surfaces and AMT-7 on the undersides. Insignia were applied in six positions: on the wing undersides, on the fuselage and on the vertical tail.

Yak-1 s/n 0636, tactical number 6, captured by the enemy at the place of forced landing, Crimea 1941. Aircraft painted in black-and-green camouflage, according to the scheme attached to the SNK Directive No.1711, insignia of enlarged size are applied in six positions.

Yak-1 from the 1st Squadron of the 8th IAP of the Black Sea Fleet Air Force, spring 1942. The airplane was painted in black-and-green camouflage, according to the scheme attached to the SNK Directive No.1711, with enlarged insignia applied in six positions.

Yak-1s from the 8th IAP of the Black Sea Fleet Air Force, flown by the Commander of the Air Force, Major-General N.A. Ostryakov, spring 1942. The airplanes were painted in black-and-green camouflage, according to the scheme applied to the SNK Directive No.1711, with enlarged insignia applied in six positions.

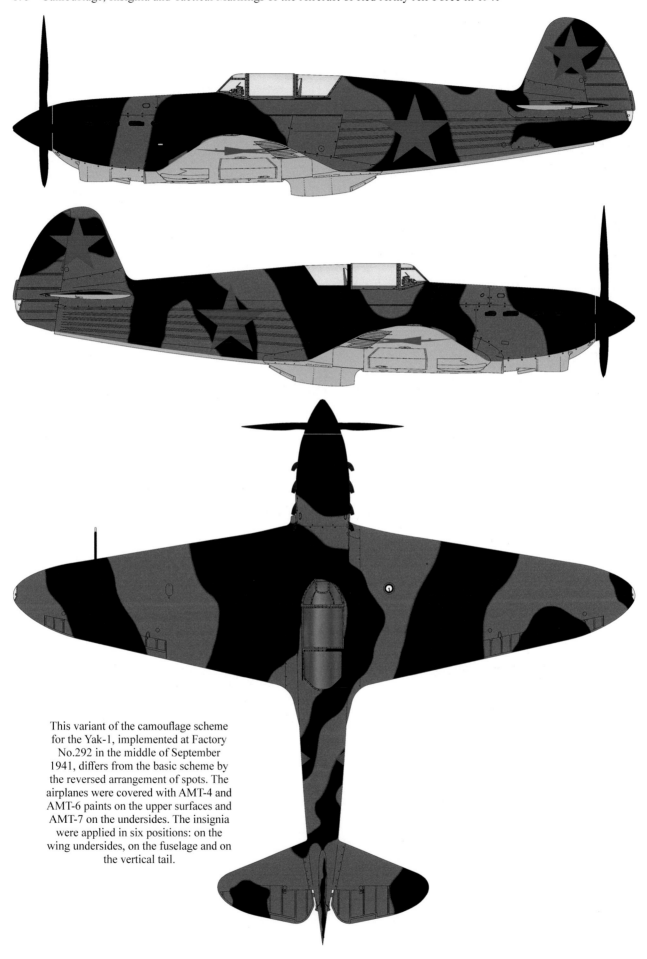

This variant of the camouflage scheme for the Yak-1, implemented at Factory No.292 in the middle of September 1941, differs from the basic scheme by the reversed arrangement of spots. The airplanes were covered with AMT-4 and AMT-6 paints on the upper surfaces and AMT-7 on the undersides. The insignia were applied in six positions: on the wing undersides, on the fuselage and on the vertical tail.

Yak-1, tactical number 8, from the 8th IAP of the Black Sea Fleet Air Force, spring 1942. The airplane was painted in black-and-green camouflage, according to the scheme attached to the SNK Directive No.1711, in alternating colours with enlarged insignia applied in six positions.

Yak-1 of the 43rd–44th series, winter 1941–1942.

Yak-1 of the 43rd–44th series, tactical number 6, captured by the enemy at the place of forced landing, winter 1941–1942. The airplane was painted in black-and-green camouflage, according to the scheme attached to the SNK Directive No.1711, with enlarged insignia applied in six positions.

Su-2 of an unknown unit, August–September 1941.

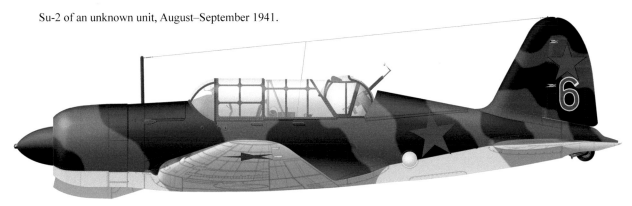

Su-2, tactical number 6, of an unknown unit, captured by the enemy at a forced landing site, August–September 1941. The airplane was painted in black-and-green camouflage, with insignia applied in six positions according to the improvised scheme of Factory No.135.

Su-2, tactical number 1, of the 43rd BAP, after forced landing, August 1941. The aircraft was painted in black-and-green camouflage, with insignia applied in six positions according to the improvised scheme of Factory No.135.

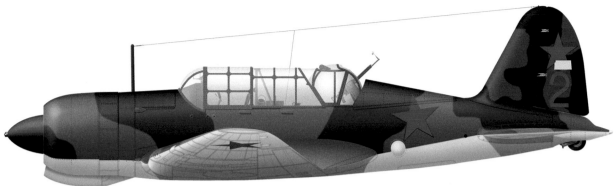

Su-2 of an unknown unit, August–September 1941.

Su-2, tactical number 2, of an unknown unit, captured by the enemy at a forced landing site, August–September 1941. The airplane was
painted in black-and-green camouflage, with insignia applied in six positions according to the improvised scheme of Factory No.135.

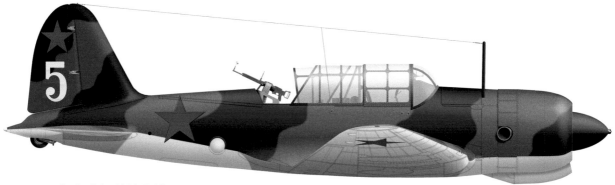

Su-2 of the 135th BAP.

Su-2, tactical number 5, of the 135th BAP. The airplane was painted in black-and-green camouflage, with insignia applied in six positions according to the improvised scheme of Factory No.135.

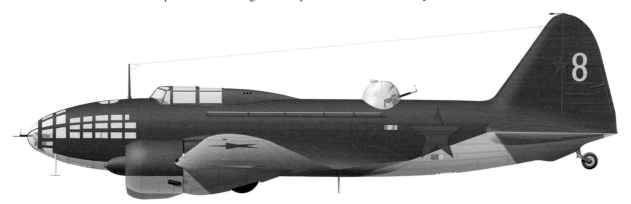

DB-3f presumably from the 52nd BAD, Orel airfield, October 1941.

DB-3f tactical number 8, presumably from the 52nd Bomber Aviation Division (BAD, *Bombardirovochnaya Aviatsionnaya Diviziya*), captured by the enemy at Orel airfield, October 1941. The airplane was painted in 'protective' green colour on the upper surfaces, with insignia applied in six positions.

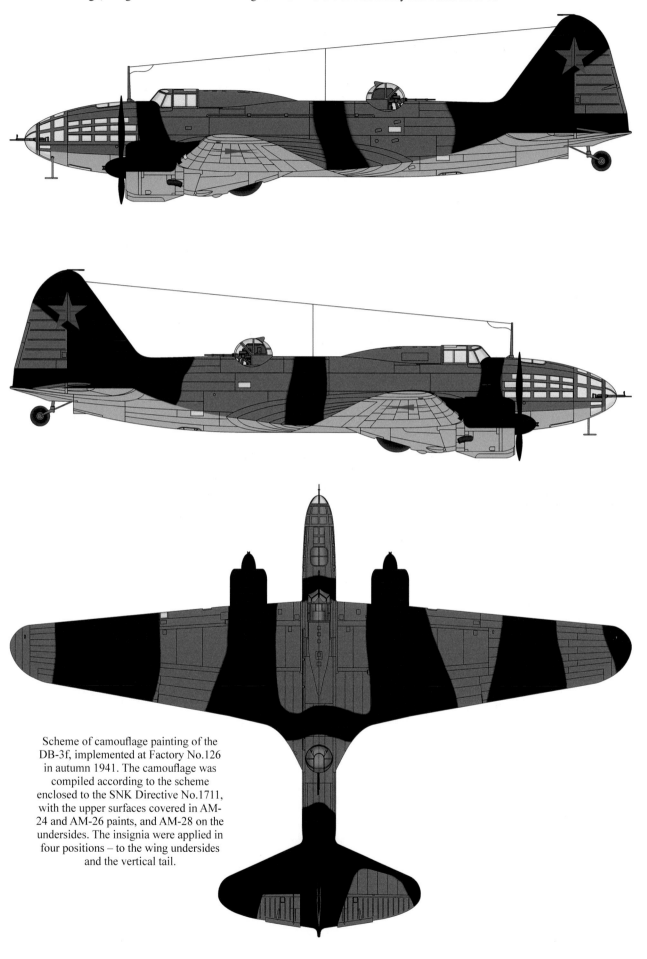

Scheme of camouflage painting of the DB-3f, implemented at Factory No.126 in autumn 1941. The camouflage was compiled according to the scheme enclosed to the SNK Directive No.1711, with the upper surfaces covered in AM-24 and AM-26 paints, and AM-28 on the undersides. The insignia were applied in four positions – to the wing undersides and the vertical tail.

DB-3f s/n A68-13, tactical number 7, with inscription 'Komsomol of Kolyma' on fuselage, from the 1st Squadron of the 98th Long-range BAP of the 52nd Long-range Aviation Division. On 27 January 1942, the airplane flown by the crew of the pilot Lieutenant S.A. Kharchenko crashed on landing at Lipetsk-2 airfield. (18)

DB-3f s/n A69-05 from the 1st Squadron of the 98th Long-range BAP of the 52nd Long-range Aviation Division, January 1942.

DB-3f s/n A69-05, tactical number 4, with inscription 'Stalin's Komsomolsk' on the fuselage, from the 1st Squadron of the 98th Long-range BAP of the 52nd Long-range Aviation Division. On 27 January 1942, the airplane flown by the crew of the pilot Lieutenant F.K. Parashchenko crashed on landing at Lipetsk-2 airfield. (19)

DB-3f, tactical number 3, with inscription 'Komsomol of Amur' on the fuselage, from the 1st Squadron of the 98th Long-range BAP of the 52nd Long-range Aviation Division, winter 1941–1942.

Assembly of Il-4 bombers of the 'Soviet Primorye' squadron at Factory No.126, Komsomolsk-on-Amur, spring 1943.

MiG-3 s/n 4809 of the 169th IAP, 3
October 1941.

MiG-3 s/n 4809, tactical number 09, of the 169th IAP. On 3 October 1941, the airplane flown by Junior Lieutenant Kalinin was lost
in a crash. The fighter was painted in monochrome 'protective' green colour on upper surfaces, with enlarged insignia applied in six
positions. (20)

MiG-3 of an unknown unit, August–
September 1941.

MiG-3 tactical number 25, of
an unknown unit, captured by
the enemy at the place of forced
landing, August–September
1941. The airplane was painted
in monochrome 'protective'
green colour on upper surfaces,
with enlarged insignia applied in
six positions.

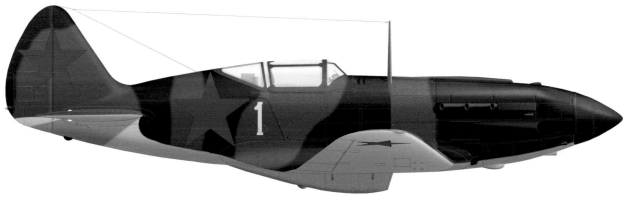

MiG-3 of an unknown unit of the Black Sea Fleet Air Force.

MiG-3 tactical number 1, of an unknown unit of the Black Sea Fleet Air Force. The airplane was painted in improvised black-and-
green camouflage on upper surfaces, and carries enlarged insignia applied in six positions.

MiG-3 s/n 3604 from the 1st Squadron of
the 425th IAP.

Crash of MiG-3 s/n 3604, tactical number 4, from the 1st Squadron of the 425th IAP. The airplane was flown by Lieutenant S.P. Zenin who perished in the crash. The fighter was painted in improvised black-and-green camouflage on upper surfaces, and carries enlarged insignia applied in six positions. (21)

TB-7s of the 432nd BAP flying on a combat mission, August–September 1941. The airplanes were painted in black-and-green camouflage in accordance with the scheme attached to the SNK Directive No.1711, with enlarged insignia applied in six positions.

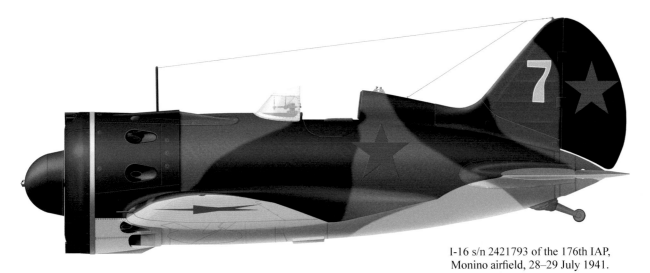

I-16 s/n 2421793 of the 176th IAP,
Monino airfield, 28–29 July 1941.

I-16 s/n 2421793, tactical number 7, of the 176th IAP, crashed on landing at Monino airfield on the night of 28–29 July. The pilot, Deputy Squadron Commander Lieutenant D.V. Stupachenko was not injured. The airplane was painted in improvised black-and-green camouflage, the insignia applied in six positions, the star on the rudder was of enlarged size, while the insignia on the fuselage remained of the earlier, smaller size. (22).

I-16 of an unknown unit, abandoned due to damage. The airplane was painted in improvised black-and-green camouflage, with insignia applied in six positions, but small in size.

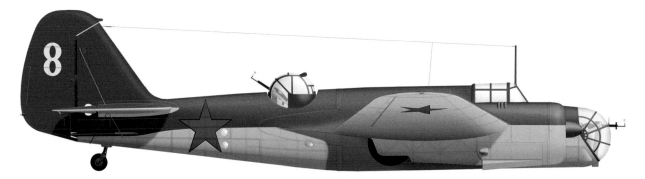

SB bomber s/n 49/8 of the 30th SBAP, Dukhovschina airfield.

SB bomber s/n 49/8, tactical number 8, of the 30th SBAP, captured by the enemy at Dukhovschina airfield. The airplane was painted in pre-war monochrome 'protective' green colour, with enlarged insignia applied, but only in four positions – on the fuselage and on the wing undersides.

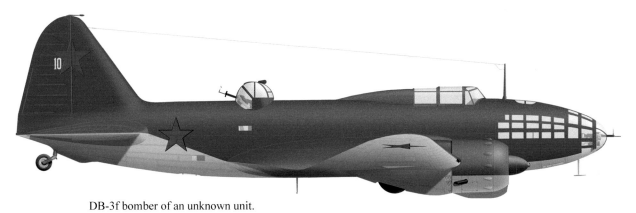

DB-3f bomber of an unknown unit.

DB-3f bomber, tactical number 10, of an unknown unit, captured by the enemy at the site of a forced landing. The airplane was painted in pre-war monochrome 'protective' green colour, but received insignia in six positions.

Repair of I-15bis fighters in autumn 1941. Note that three airplanes are painted differently – the farthest has black-and-green camouflage, the next one has a star on the tailfin, and the third features enlarged insignia on the fuselage.

SB s/n 5/Б of the 15th Separate Reconnaissance Aviation Squadron of the Central Asian Military District Air Force. On 13 August 1941, the bomber flown by the crew of the pilot Sergeant V.I. Ivlev crashed at Karshi airfield. The airplane was painted in black-and-green camouflage, according to the scheme attached to the SNK Directive No.1711, with insignia applied in four positions; the stars on the fuselage and wing upper surfaces were painted over. (23)

I-153 s/n 6853 from the 4th Squadron of the 152nd IAP, Kegostrov airfield, 10 August 1941.

I-153 s/n 6853, tactical number 12, from the 4th Squadron of the 152nd IAP. On 10 August 1941, the fighter flown by the Wing Commander, Lieutenant I.N. Galoshin crashed at Kegostrov airfield. The airplane had been repainted – the upper surfaces in green, the undersides in blue, the insignia on the wing upper surfaces were painted over, but on the vertical tail they were not applied at all. (24).

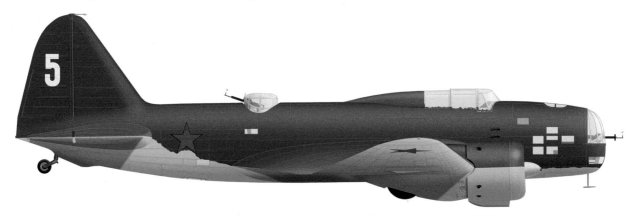

DB-3 bomber s/n 180203 of the 139th SBAP, Taisin airfield, 6 August 1941.

DB-3 bomber s/n 180203, tactical number 5, of the 139th SBAP. On 6 August 1941, the bomber flown by the crew of the pilot Deputy Regimental Commander, Major S.A. Gelbach crashed at Taisin airfield. The airplane had been repainted – the upper surfaces in green, the undersides in blue, the insignia remained in six positions according to the pre-war standard. (25).

I-16 type 29 of the 167th IAP, autumn 1941.

I-16 type 29, tactical number 30, of the 167th IAP, autumn 1941. The aircraft was repainted in silver colour, the insignia remained in six positions according to the pre-war standard.

I-16 type 29 s/n 2921356 from the 3rd Squadron of the 167th IAP, 137th SAD, 24 November 1941.

I-16 type 29 s/n 2921356, tactical number 15, from the 3rd Squadron of the 167th IAP, 137th SAD. On 24 November 1941, the fighter flown by Junior Lieutenant Kovalyonok crashed on landing at Mashhad airfield. The airplane was repainted in silver colour, the insignia remained in six positions according to the pre-war standard.

I-153 s/n 8791 of the 492nd ShAP, Mashhad airfield, 16 December 1941.

I-153 s/n 8791, tactical number 20, of the 492nd ShAP. On 16 December 1941, the fighter flown by Squadron Commander Lieutenant P.S. Lembek crashed at Mashhad airfield. The airplane was repainted in silver colour, the insignia remained in six positions according to the pre-war standard. (26)

5

Winter Camouflage

Up until the winter of 1941–42 the winter camouflage had not been used on the airplanes of the VVS RKKA on a mass scale. However, the work on the creation of white paint, as well as the winter camouflage schemes had been conducted at least since 1935. The camouflaging white paint created by VIAM was tested by the 5th Department of the NII VVS and was found suitable for application. These events are described in detail in the publication by V. Vakhlamov and M. Orlov 'Colours of Soviet Aviation' (1).

Probably one of the first documents regulating the application of white camouflage appeared during the Soviet-Finnish War. It was the 'Instruction on camouflage of operational airfields of active armies in the winter period', approved by the Air Force Order No.14 dated 31 January 1940. This instruction describes the types of winter camouflage application. Depending on the forestless or wooded terrain, it was recommended to apply either single-coloured white camouflage, or mixed camouflage (when the basic colour of the aircraft camouflage was amended with white spots). The schemes of the spots application were presented for the TB-3, SB, R-5, and I-16 aircraft. (2) It should be noted that the instruction was developed by one of the future creators of the 'three-colour' camouflages of 1941 and 1943, a Military Engineer 2nd rank E.Z. Yasin. The temporary white camouflaging paint was developed in VIAM, by the coryphaeus of creating the paints for the VVS RKKA, engineer V.V. Chebotarevskiy – it was a mixture of zinc white, chalk and casein glue.

However, for various reasons it was then impossible to implement the instructions about camouflage painting of airplanes though the document was printed in a substantial circulation in 420 copies.

However, the experts managed to test out their theoretical developments and check the white camouflage paint on 1–12 March 1940 at the combat unit. The letter of 8 April 1940 sent to the leadership of VIAM, signed by the Deputy Head of the Rear of the VVS RKKA Headquarters and the chief engineer on camouflaging, reported about the tests of the white camouflage paint created by engineer Chebotarevskiy and gave the following evaluation: *In general the paint has shown positive results and will be applied in the future*'. (3) Basing on the results, the following positive properties were noted: '*the possibility of quick application on the surface of the aircraft; durability (during combat flights the paint did not flake or crumble); good camouflaging effect*'. Some technical disadvantages were also noted and the following wishes were expressed for eliminating them: '*to get the paint not in the form of paste, but in a dry or powder state to avoid its freezing and to eliminate unnecessary weight while transporting; to include a fixer in its composition for the possibility of immediate use when diluting the paint with water. (4)

This experiment undoubtedly played an extremely positive role. Its results were immediately used in further developments: for example, the use of zinc and lead whites was found unacceptable because it gave a spectrum of reflection very different from that of snow in the ultraviolet range. By the difficult winter of 1941, the VVS RKKA had adopted the use of white camouflage paint MK-7.

The MK-7 paint consisted of a base (chalk, diluted with water and alcohol, and added 0.1-0.2 % of ultramarine to neutralize the yellowing of the chalk) and a fixer (casein glue mixed with water).

The methods of preparing the paint and applying it to aircraft were described in detail in the publication of V. Vakhlamov and M. Orlov based on documents of the NII VVS:

According to the instruction approved on 12 October 1941, all upper and side surfaces, except for the insignia, were to be completely covered with paint. Dirty and peeled areas were to be renewed periodically. The paint was applied in two layers with a spray gun or in 1–2 layers with a brush directly over the summer camouflage on the upper and side surfaces. The applied paint layer had to be even, without roughness and 'slightly translucent with the main paint coating.

Camouflaging of one fighter airplane required about 6kg of MK-7 paste, 9kg was needed for the Il-2, 15kg for the Il-4 or SB, 23kg for the Li-2, 8kg for the U-2, and 35kg for the Pe-8.

In addition to chalk paint MK-7 there were its modifications MK-7Sh (МК-7Ш) based on gypsum, and MK-7F (МК-7Ф) – chalk diluted with water with alcohol and formalin. Due to the shortage of chalk, there were developed and tested in

January 1942 other white washable paints: C-1, C-4a, Б, АБ-1 which used alabaster, lime or gypsum as a white pigment. Nevertheless, MK-7 remained the main one. (5)

Transition to the winter camouflage took place in November 1941, and, of course, it didn't happen simultaneously: the timing varied greatly at different sections of the front, and even in the units of the same formation. Application of the winter camouflage was first noted in the accident report of the 26th IAP of the 7th IAK, Leningrad Air Defense Forces, filed on 14 November 1941. The pictures clearly show a carefully painted white MiG-3 fighter airplane of the early series. In addition to the photos from the accident reports, there are a profusion of photos of aircraft of the Air Forces of the Northern Front and the Red-Banner Baltic Fleet. Practically all airplanes had thoroughly applied winter camouflage; however, due to the lack of documented facts it is impossible to define what paints were used except for the MK-7 paint. There is a high probability that white nitro lacquers II were used as some of the aircraft in the photos have a distinctive gloss finish. Insignia on most of the aircraft were applied in six positions, but not all airplanes had the approved enlarged ones. There are also noted airplanes with pre-war schemes of insignia application, with fuselage stars of smaller size and insignia applied in four positions according to the SNK Directive No.1711 of 20 June 1941. The camouflaging of the airplanes of the Air Forces of the North Fleet and Red-Banner Baltic Fleet arouses interest since the majority of aircraft captured by cameras were used in combats of summer – autumn 1941. These airplanes were mostly painted in the combat units, and to a lesser degree in stationary workshops, repair bases and at Factory No.47.

On the Western and Kalinin Fronts, as well as in the 6th IAK of the Moscow Air Defense Forces, most aircraft were also completely painted into the white camouflage. As in the case of the Northern Front, there is no information in the records of units and formations about the paints used – MK-7 or nitro lacquer. Judging by photos, both variants were applied. The regiments arriving from interior districts, armed with the obsolete aircraft types (R-5, R-Zet, U-2, I-16 type 5, I-15bis and I-5), were also instructed to repaint the airplanes into the white camouflage. The modern P-40 fighters that had been allocated to the 126th IAP of the Air Defense Forces were painted in white as well. The distinctive feature of the airplanes of the 6th IAK of the Air Defense Forces is the strict adherence to the instructions – the enlarged insignia were applied in six positions.

The situation with aircraft camouflaging was similar at the Southwestern and Southern Fronts. And similarly, there is almost no information about the type of paint used. Nevertheless, both the airplanes of the rear regiments arriving to the Fronts and the combat airplanes which remained there since the summer – autumn 1941 were mandatorily repainted in the white camouflage.

Unlike their colleagues from the front-line aviation, units of the long-range aviation armed with DB-3, DB-3f and TB-3 airplanes had almost completely switched to night operations by the winter of 1941–1942. Therefore, there was obviously no urgent need to paint airplanes in white camouflage. Nevertheless, in many regiments the task was completed.

It should be noted that Air Force units in rear districts, Transcaucasian and Central Asian Military Districts did not transfer to the winter camouflage at all. In the meantime, the Air Forces of the Far Eastern Front and probably of the Transbaikal Military District, though partially but repainted the airplanes in the white camouflage and did it simultaneously with the combating Air Force in November 1941.

Similarly to the case with the application of black-and-green camouflages, for various reasons, such as shortage of paint, limited time, etc, the airplanes were often painted partially – with large fragments not covered properly.

There were also exceptions. For example, MiG-3 fighters of the 39th IAD were covered with white paint in patches, thus forming an improvised winter camouflage. The shape of the spots and colour combinations depended on the aircraft original colouring, the skill of the technicians, and the properties of the white paint used.

It should be noted that, as it was expected: *[T]he MK-7 paint coating was quite destroyable and, if the instructions for renewing the paint were not followed, gradually wore off, more and more exposing the summer paint: the so-called 'spring' camouflage appeared on the aircraft by the end of winter all by itself.* (14)

In some units the regulations were not strictly followed, and the winter camouflage was not being renewed. As a result, by spring many airplanes looked untidy and exotic. The white paint was peeling off, primarily from the nose section, revealing black-and-green camouflage. The documents dispassionately noted that the 'winter' painting reduced the aerodynamic properties of the airplanes:

Depending on the size of chalk particles, the winter camouflage 'ate up' from 10 to 25km/h of airspeed. Therefore, during MK-7 preparation it was important to strictly follow the technological process, which was not always the case. In November 1942 at the Factory No.36 a batch of this paint was rejected because the chalk was not properly sifted. Loss of speed could be substantially reduced or even completely eliminated by treating the painted surfaces with sandpaper Nos.1, 00, 000 or even just with a rough rag over the just-dried layer, but such measures in the front-line conditions were hardly realistic. (13)

Besides, some airplanes were not repainted at all for one reason or another. A number of photos show airplanes of different schemes in the same unit: for example, on the well-known image of presenting the Guards Banner to the personnel of the 12th Guards IAP, three aircraft were not painted in the white camouflage at all out of the line of ten MiG-3 fighters, and one airplane had the outer wing panels not covered in white after repair.

At the NKAP factories, repainting into winter camouflage was better organized. Unfortunately, due to the difficult situation caused by the evacuation of some factories and the increase of production at other ones there is not much information remaining in the factory records about the transition to winter camouflage. At the present time, such records were found only in the documents of the Factory No.292. The report of military acceptance says that, firstly, the task of winter camouflage painting was set in November 1941, secondly, they tried but failed to produce the MK-7 type paint directly at the factory, and thirdly, the factory was covering the aircraft with nitro paint, the designation of which is unknown:

Winter camouflage of the airplanes was finally implemented starting from 29 November, the painting was done with white nitro paint produced by our factory and since 29 November all the airplanes were directed to the units with winter camouflage, however, it led to the necessity of repainting all the airplanes stationed at the airfield.

Prior to that the factory tried to create winter camouflage with casein-glue-based washed-off white paint, but the experience of operating several airplanes covered with this paint showed its complete unsuitability and the airplanes had to be repainted by the factory.' (15)

The pilots of the 10th, 66th, 236th, 237th, 296th, 211th and 562nd IAPs were the first to receive aircraft with the winter camouflage (16). Judging by the clearly attributed photos of the aircraft from the 66th, 236th, and 562nd IAPs, the airplanes had been completely painted with an even layer, i.e. obviously the paint was applied with a spray gun. The insignia were applied in six positions, and tactical numbers were painted in the rear parts of the fuselages.

Some information about painting LaGG-3s at Factory No.21 can be found in the accident reports for the airplanes that crashed during acceptance at the factory airfield and from the photos taken at the 2nd ZAP where most of the regiments were converted to the LaGG-3s. The accident reports show that, at least from December 1941 until the end of March 1942, the airplanes at Factory No.21 were rolled out in white camouflage, with enlarged insignia in six positions.

The Moscow-based factories, which were involved in repairing the aircraft, became another supplier of the airplanes painted in winter camouflage. Numerous photos were taken at Factory No.30, and apparently some pictures were assembled at Factories Nos.39 and 301. The photos show the repair of MiG-3, I-16, Il-2 and Pe-3 aircraft. It is clearly seen that the combat aircraft were painted differently at different enterprises, and obviously with different paint types, both MK-7 and white nitro lacquer II.

Unfortunately, information from most of the factories as to how the airplanes were painted during the winter of 1941–42 is not available. It should be noted, however, that by December 1941 the process of aircraft repainting, both at the frontline and at the factories, apparently have gained momentum, proven by the fact that the majority of the airplanes captured in photos and newsreels were already camouflaged in white, which was important given the difficult situation at the front. Despite the defeats at Rostov, Tikhvin, Kalinin and Moscow, Luftwaffe remained a dangerous enemy and took advantage of any, even the slightest negligence in camouflaging. Thus, between 27 January and 4 February 1942 Luftwaffe destroyed 69 (including nine TB-3s and nine PS-84s) and damaged ten (including three TB-3s and one PS-84s) airplanes at the airfields of Grabtsevo, Rzhavets, Zhashkovo and Oreshkovo (near Kaluga) from the group preparing an assault airdrop in the Vyazma region. The commission investigating the causes of this accident attributed this failure to the absence of camouflage paint on the large PS-84 and TB-3 airplanes that made the airfields de-masked and exposed to bombing attacks. (19)

In conclusion, it should be noted some specifics of applying tactical markings. The first variant was to leave the old number and a part of 'summer' paint around it, usually of a round or oval shape. The second option was applying a small tactical number next to the one that had been painted over. And the third, quite a notable variant involved application of the number over the insignia on the tail.

A specific feature of the camouflage in winter of 1941–42 was significant number of patriotic inscriptions and slogans applied on the airplanes. This process had begun in summer, however, during the Battle for Moscow the number of photos of airplanes with inscriptions 'For the Motherland' or 'For Stalin' went up for obvious reasons.

In addition to patriotic inscriptions, there were aircraft with dedicatory inscriptions, mainly from the labor collectives who contributed money for manufacturing of combat aircraft. The most notable airplanes with such inscriptions are probably the DB-3f bombers built in December 1941 at Factory No.126 in Komsomolsk-on-Amur, which were manufactured using the funds collected by the Komsomol members of the Far East. The aircraft carried the inscriptions 'Komsomol of Kolyma,' 'Stalin's Komsomolsk' and ' Komsomol of Khabarovsk ' as well as stylized lightning bolts along the entire fuselage. The bombers do not feature winter camouflage, which indicates that Factory No.126 at that time had not yet covered the aircraft with white paint. Unfortunately, the records of the 98th Long-range BAP, which received the donated airplanes, give no information whether they were later painted in the white 'winter' camouflage. However, it would have been a pity to hide such beautiful inscriptions and 'lightning bolts' under the dull white paint.

List of documents employed:

1. V. Vakhlamov, M. Orlov, 'Colours of Soviet Aviation'. *M-Hobby* magazine. Issues 8/1997–5/1999.
2. Ibid
3. Samara branch of the РГАНТД. Ф. Р-124. Оп. 1–6. Д. 86. л. 38.
4. Ibid
5. V. Vakhlamov, M. Orlov, 'Colours of Soviet Aviation'. *M-Hobby* magazine. Issue 2/1999.
6. ЦАМО, ф.12294, д. 49, л.156–165.
7. ЦАМО, ф.12294, д. 49, л.196–205.
8. ЦАМО, ф.286-го ИАП, оп. 143480, д.1, л.62об.
9. ЦАМО, ф.34-го гвБАП, оп. 143420, д.1, л.82–83.
10. ЦАМО, ф.12290, д.162, л.79–93.
11. ЦАМО, ф.12290, д.162, л.38–50.
12. ЦАМО, ф.12294, д.184, л.193–209.
13. V. Vakhlamov, M. Orlov, 'Colours of Soviet Aviation'. *M-Hobby* magazine. Issue 2/1999.
14. Ibid
15. ЦАМО, ф.35, оп.11605, д.5120, л.84–85.
16. ЦАМО, ф.35, оп.11605, д.5116, л.18–20.
17. ЦАМО, ф.35, оп.11605, д.1180, л.27–40.
18. ЦАМО, ф.35, оп.11605, д.1180, л.116–126.
19. ЦАМО, ф.208, оп.2589, д.157, л.7–20.
20. ЦАМО, ф.9-го гвБАП, оп. 364097, д.1, л.153.

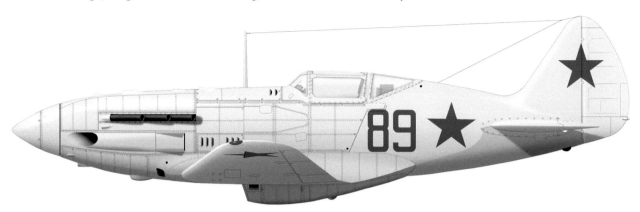

MiG-3 s/n 2289 from the 2nd Squadron of the 26th IAP, 14 November 1941.

MiG-3 s/n 2289, tactical number 89, from the 2nd Squadron of the 26th IAP, flown by the Deputy Squadron Commander Lieutenant
V.A. Koren. The airplane crashed on landing on 14 November 1941.

I-16 type 29 s/n 2921252 from the 2nd Squadron of the
123rd IAP, 5 December 1941.

I-16 type 29 s/n 2921252, tactical number 52, from the 2nd Squadron of the 123rd IAP, flown by Squadron Commander Lieutenant
I.D. Pidtykan. The airplane crashed due to engine malfunction on 5 December 1941.

MiG-3 of the 124th IAP, winter 1941–1942.

The pilots of the 124th IAP, with the MiG-3 in the background, winter 1941–1942. The aircraft of the late series, tactical number 44.

I-16 type 5 of an unknown unit, 10 December 1941.

I-16 type 5, tactical number 64, of an unknown unit which was improved by installation of four rocket projectiles and windscreen of the late series. It was discovered on 10 December 1941 on the ice of Ladoga Lake near Kexholm and captured by Finnish troops.

I-16 type 24 of the 286th IAP, winter 1941–1942.

Commander of the 286th IAP Lieutenant Colonel P.N. Baranov near I-16 type 24, tactical number 22, winter 1941–1942. (8)

LaGG-3 of an unknown unit, February 1942.

LaGG-3, tactical number 29, of an unknown unit was discovered in February 1942 on the ice of Ladoga Lake and captured by Finnish army. It was restored afterwards and used by the Finnish Air Force with LG-1 registration number.

LaGG-3 of an unknown unit, 20 February 1942.

LaGG-3, tactical number 33, presumably built by the Factory No.23. The aircraft was discovered on 20 February 1942 in the vicinity of Vidlitsa (35km to the north of Olonets) and captured by Finnish troops. Later it was restored and used in the Finnish Air Force with LG-2 registration number.

LaGG-3 presumably from the 11th Guards IAP of the 7th IAK of the Air Defense Forces, spring 1942.

LaGG-3, tactical number 46, presumably from the 11th Guards IAP of the 7th IAK of the Air Defense Forces, spring 1942.

Above and right: I-15bis presumably from the Leningrad Front Air Force, winter 1941–1942.

Above and right: SB bomber from the 44th SBAP of the 2nd SAD of the Leningrad Front Air Force, Kavgolovskoye Lake airfield, winter 1941–42. (9)

Left and below: MiG-3 of the 6th IAK of the Air Defense Forces, winter 1941–42. The airplane upper surfaces were painted in white throughout, the enlarged insignia were applied in six positions.

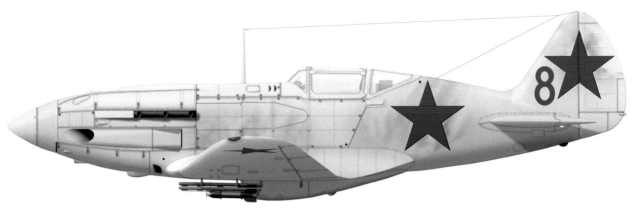

Above and right: MiG-3 from the 27th IAP of the 6th IAK of the Air Defense Forces, winter 1941–42.

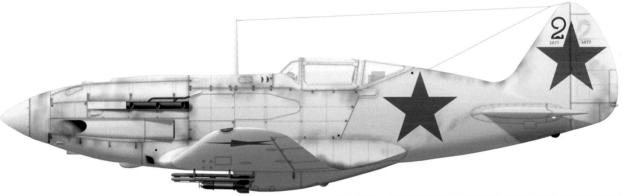

Above and right: MiG-3 s/n 5077 from the 28th IAP of the 6th IAK of the Air Defense Forces, winter 1941–42.

Forced landing of the Yak-1 from the 562nd IAP of the 6th IAK of the Air Defense Forces, winter 1941–42.

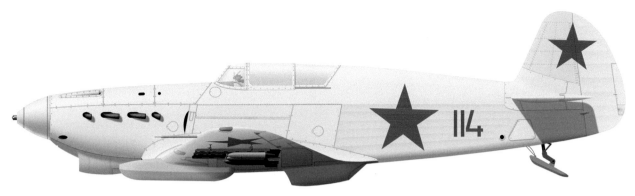

Yak-1 from the 236th IAP of the Western Front Air Force, airfield near Mozhaisk, January 1942.

Pilots from the 236th IAP of the Western Front Air Force at the airfield near Mozhaisk with Yak-1 fighters in the background, January 1942. From left to right: Lieutenant A. Maksimov, Senior Lieutenants M. Lipin and P. Medvedev, Battalion Commissar S. Rogozhnikov.

Pilots in front of the I-153 from the 120th IAP of the 6th IAK of the Air Defense Forces, winter 1941–42. The airplane upper surfaces were painted entirely in white, enlarged insignia were applied in six positions.

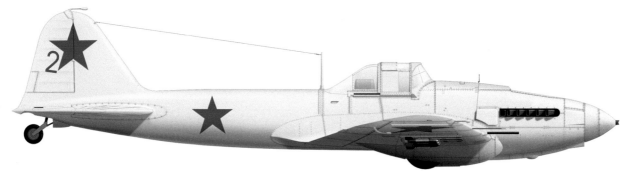

Above: Il-2 from the 765th ShAP of the Western Front Air Force, winter 1941–42.
Right: Il-2, tactical number 2, from the 765th ShAP of the Western Front Air Force before combat mission, winter 1941–42.
Below: Il-2, tactical number 4, presumably from the 62nd ShAP of the 77th SAD captured by the enemy at the place of forced landing, winter 1941–42.

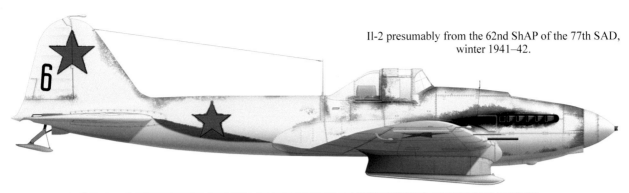

Il-2 presumably from the 62nd ShAP of the 77th SAD,
winter 1941–42.

Above: Il-2, tactical number 6, presumably from the 62nd
ShAP of the 77th SAD, winter 1941–42.
Right: Pe-3, tactical number 3, from the 95th IAP of the 6th
IAK of the Air Defense Forces in flight, winter 1941–42.

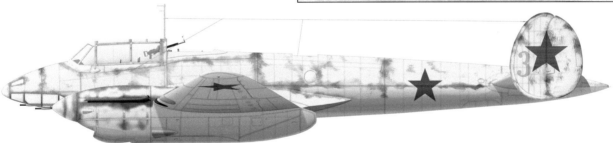

Pe-3 from the 95th IAP of the 6th IAK of the Air Defense Forces, winter 1941–1942.

Pe-3 presumably from the 95th IAP of 6th IAK of the Air Defense Forces, winter 1941–42.

Pe-2 during tests of the ski landing gear, winter 1941–42.

Pe-2s, tactical numbers 2 and 21, from the 130th BAP of the Western Front Air Force at the airfield, winter 1941–42.

A pilot from the 188th IAP of the 77th SAD of the Western Front Air Force, Junior Lieutenant E.P. Popov in the cockpit of I-15bis, winter 1941–42.

A pilot from the 188th IAP of the 77th SAD of the Western Front Air Force, Lieutenant N.A. Secheyko, in the cockpit of I-5 fighter, winter 1941–42.

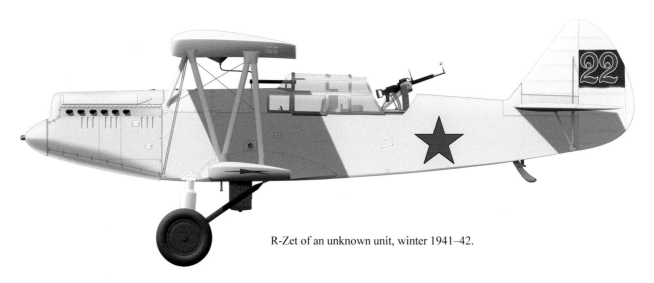

R-Zet of an unknown unit, winter 1941–42.

R-Zet shot down in the vicinity of Istra – Burzhatovo, winter 1941–1942.

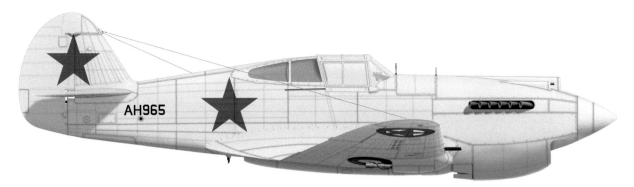

P-40 from the 126th IAP of the 6th IAK, Air Defense Forces, winter 1941–42.

P-40 fighter from the 126th IAP of the 6th IAK of the Air Defense Forces, winter 1941–42.

Top left: I-16 type 24 from the 43rd IAP of the Southwestern Front Air Force, winter 1941–42. The airplane was painted with white nitro paint overall, enlarged insignia were refreshed and received black trim.

Top right: I-16 type 17 from the 40th IAP of the Southwestern Front Air Force, winter 1941–42.

Left: Deputy Squadron Commander of the 16th Guards IAP, 20th IAD of the South Front Air Force, Senior Lieutenant A.I. Pokryshkin near the MiG-3, winter 1941–42.

Below: Pilots from the 23rd IAP of the Southern Front Air Force next to the Yak-1 fighter, winter 1941–42.

Bottom left: I-15bis presumably from the Southwestern Front Air Force, winter 1941–42.

Bottom right: Crew of the Su-2, tactical number 2, from the 210th BAP of the Southern Front Air Force, winter 1941–42.

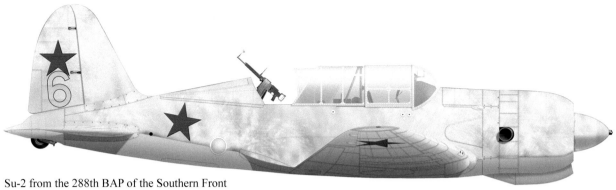

Su-2 from the 288th BAP of the Southern Front
Air Force, 4 February 1942.

Forced landing of the Su-2, tactical
number 6, from the 288th BAP of the
Southern Front Air Force, 4 February
1942. The aircraft was hit by German
fighters, the pilot Junior Lieutenant
Nikolayev and the navigator Sergeant
Andreev died.

Formation of Pe-2 bombers, presumably of the Southern Front Air Force, winter 1941–1942.

DB-3f s/n 181513 from the 3rd Squadron of the 83rd Long-range BAP of the 40th Long-range Air Division, Isanino airfield (Rybinsk), 28 January 1942.

Crash landing of the DB-3f s/n 181513 from the 3rd Squadron of the 83rd Long-range BAP of the 40th Long-range Air Division, Isanino airfield (Rybinsk), 28 January 1942. The crew of Sergeant Major V.F. Tarasychev. The airplane was painted in white camouflage overall, with small insignia applied in six positions. (10)

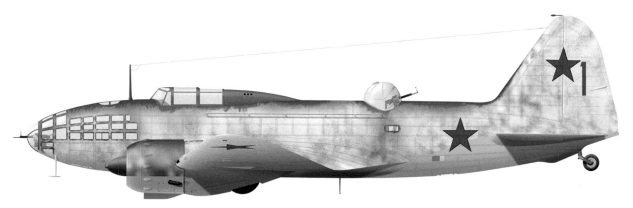

DB-3f s/n 391904 from the 3rd Squadron of the 7th Long-range BAP, 40th Long-range Air Division, 20 January 1942.

Crash of a DB-3f s/n 391904 from the 3rd Squadron of the 7th Long-range BAP of the 40th Long-range Air Division, near Abramovo village (Murom region, 12km southwest of Lopatino airfield), 20 January 1942. The pilot, Lieutenant K.P. Prokofyev and the navigator, Junior Lieutenant Kukarskiy died. (11)

Left: The crew of the pilot Senior Lieutenant P.T. Ananyev in front of the TB-3 from the 1st Guards Aviation Regiment of the 23rd Long-range Air Division, spring 1942. The airplane was equipped with MV-3 turrets and painted in white overall.
Right: The crew of the pilot Captain V.P. Filin in front of the TB-3 from 1st Guards Aviation Regiment of the 23rd Long-range Air Division, spring 1942. The airplane was painted in white overall.

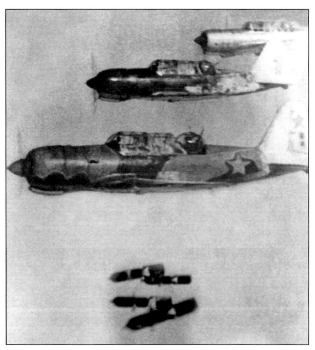

Il-2 of an unknown unit, winter 1941–42.

Formation of Su-2 bombers from one of the regiments of the Southern Front Air Force, winter 1941–42.

Pilots from the 728th IAP of the Western Front Air Force near the I-16 type 10 fighter, winter 1941–42.

A pilot from the 53rd IAP of the 34th SAD of the Far Eastern Front Air Force, Lieutenant V.P. Gavrish, near the I-153 covered with white paint, winter 1941–42.

Crash of I-15bis s/n 4797 from the 2nd Squadron of the 583rd IAP, 69th SAD of the Far Eastern Front Air Force, 27 November 1941. The airplane was painted white overall, with smaller insignia applied in four positions according to the Directive No.1711 of 20 June 1941.

Pilots of the 23rd IAP of the Southern Front Air Force near a LaGG-3 fighter, winter 1941–42.

I-16 type 10 from the 728th IAP of the Western
Front Air Force, winter 1941–42.

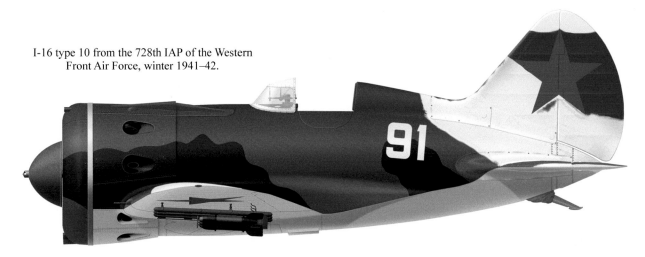

MiG-3, tactical number 60, from the
Staff Flight of the 39th IAD of the
Southern Front Air Force. The airplane
was painted in the improvised winter
camouflage of irregularly shaped white
spots over the basic black-and-green
camouflage, winter 1941–42.

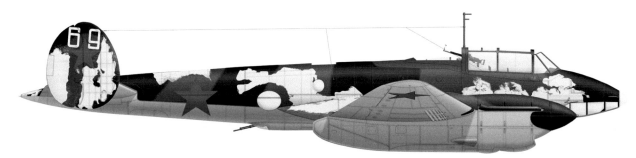

Pe-2 from the 5th SBAP of the Southern Front Air Force, winter 1941–42.

Pe-2 bomber, tactical number 69, from the 5th SBAP of the Southern Front Air Force. The airplane was painted in the improvised
winter camouflage of irregularly shaped white spots over the basic black-and-green camouflage, winter 1941–42.

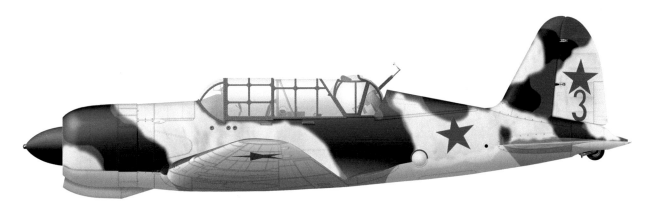

Su-2 from the 2nd Squadron of the 210th BAP of the Southern Front Air Force, winter 1941–42.

Su-2, tactical number 3, from the 2nd Squadron of the 210th BAP of the Southern Front Air Force. The airplane was painted in the improvised winter camouflage of irregularly shaped white spots over the basic black-and-green camouflage, winter 1941–42.

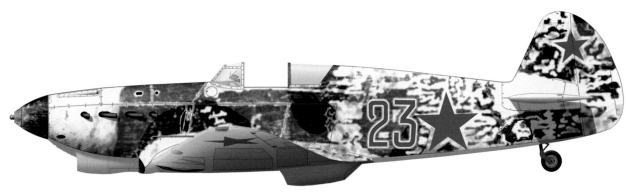

Yak-1 s/n 0506 from the 123rd IAP of the 7th IAK of the Air Defense Forces, 23 April 1942.

Yak-1 s/n 0506 from the 123rd IAP of the 7th IAK of the Air Defense Forces, flown by Captain G.N. Zhidov, 23 April 1942. The wear of winter camouflage is clearly seen, the paint on the nose part is almost completely peeled off.

MiG-3 from the 122nd IAP of the Western Front Air Force, flown by Lieutenant Yu.B. Alekseev, winter 1941–42.

I-16 of an unknown unit, winter 1941–42.

Presentation of the Guards Banner to the personnel of the 12th Guards IAP of the 6th IAK of the Air Defense Forces, against the background of lined-up MiG-3 fighters, March 1942.

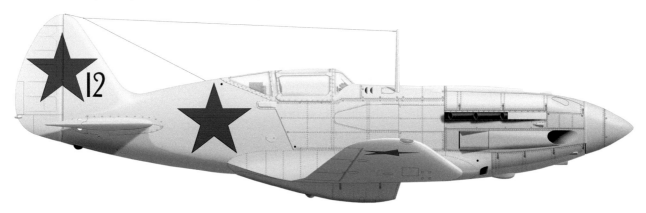

MiG-3 from the 12th Guards IAP of the 6th IAK of the Air Defense Forces, March 1942.

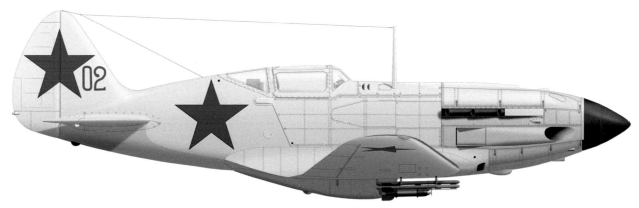

MiG-3 from the 12th Guards IAP of the 6th IAK of the Air Defense Forces, March 1942.

Pilots of the 66th IAP of the Western Front Air Force near Yak-1 fighter, winter 1941–42.

Pilots of the 562nd IAP, 6th IAK of the Air Defense Forces, near Yak-1 fighter, winter 1941–42.

Yak-1 fighter of an unknown unit, winter 1941–42.

Yak-1 fighter, tactical number 73, of an unknown unit, captured by the enemy at the place of forced landing, winter 1941–42.

Yak-1 fighter of an unknown unit, captured by the enemy at the place of forced landing, winter 1941–42.

LaGG-3 of the 737th IAP at Savasleika airfield during conversion training at the 2nd ZAP, December 1941.

Crash of the LaGG-3 s/n 312119-21 at the airfield of Factory No.21 due to the engine failure during the acceptance test flight on 25 January 1942.

Crash of the LaGG-3 s/n 312124-57 at the airfield of Factory No.21 due to the engine failure during the acceptance test flight on 25 March 1942.

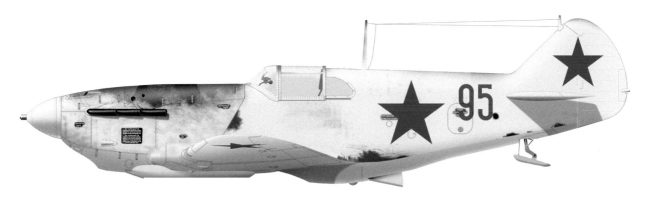

LaGG-3 of the 19th IAP, Savasleika airfield, February 1942.

LaGG-3 fighter, tactical number 95, of the 19th IAP at Savasleika airfield during conversion training at the 2nd ZAP, February 1942.

LaGG-3 of the 255th IAP at Savasleika airfield, during conversion training at the 2nd ZAP. Note that although the photo was taken in March 1942, the aircraft was still equipped with ski landing gear.

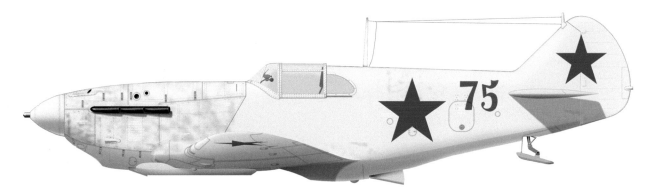

LaGG-3 of an unknown unit, March 1942.

LaGG-3, tactical number 75, of an unknown unit, captured by the enemy at the place of forced landing, March 1942. Note that the aircraft is still equipped with ski landing gear.

Previous page bottom image and this page: MiG-3, I-16, Il-2 and Pe-3 aircraft in course of repair at factories in Moscow, winter 1941–42.

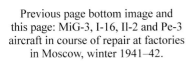

Personnel near the tail of the DB-3f bomber of the 51st Long-range BAP, winter 1941–1942. Note the tactical number 21 applied over the insignia. (20)

Yak-1 of an unknown unit which was shot down over the enemy-occupied territory. Note tactical number 9 applied over the insignia, winter 1941–42.

Repair of the I-16 at Factory No.30 in Moscow. Note tactical number 6 is applied over the insignia, winter 1941–42.

MiG-3 of the 122nd IAP, Western Front Air Force, winter 1941–1942.

Handing over the airplanes to the personnel of the 122nd IAP of the Western Front Air Force. The MiG-3 fighters feature 'arrows' and slogans: 'For the Motherland', 'For Stalin', 'For the Bolshevik Party', winter 1941–42.

Preparation for a mission of the MiG-3 fighter from the 148th IAP of the Southwestern Front Air Force, winter 1941–42. Note the inscription 'For Stalin' applied over the insignia.

Senior Political Instructor Panov of the 43rd IAP of the Southwestern Front Air Force near the I-16 fighter, winter 1941–42. Note the inscription 'For the Motherland'.

Il-2s from the 7th Guards ShAP of the Southern Front Air Force, March 1942. Note the inscription 'Fight for the Motherland' and 'Death to fascist invaders!'.

Squadron Commander of the 7th Guards ShAP of the Southern Front Air Force, Captain N.A. Zub, setting a task to the personnel near the Il-2, March 1942. Note the inscription 'Death to fascist invaders!' on the fuselage.

LaGG-3 of the 10th IAP, March 1942.

Above and left: Squadron Commander of the 10th IAP Senior Lieutenant S.L. Maksimenko in the cockpit of the LaGG-3 carrying the individual name 'Gorky Pioneer' and a dedicatory inscription 'Gift to the Glorious Soviet Pilots of the VVS RKKA from the Pioneer Organization of the Gorky Region', March 1942.

DB-3f with inscription 'Khabarovsk Komsomol' before being transferred to the 1st Squadron of the 98th Long-range BAP, 52nd Aviation Division, winter 1941–42.